INEFFABLE ATTRIBUTES

UNDERSTANDING THE INCONCEIVABLE
CHARACTERISTICS OF GOD

JUDAH VERITAS

ACKNOWLEDGMENTS

To the Trinitarian God – Heavenly Father, the Son – the Lord Jesus Christ, and the Holy Spirit – for all that He has done and given me. Anything that has been edifying and profitable is by His Wisdom alone.

To my spiritual fathers from afar – David Wilkerson, Leonard Ravenhill, and A.W. Tozer – for convicting me of my sin and lighting a fire inside my soul for Truth.

To my deceased dog, Buddy, who sat beside me and gave me company as I wrote.

"Indeed these are the mere edges of His ways,
And how small a whisper we hear of Him!
But the thunder of His power who can understand?"

— Job 26:14 NKJV

CONTENTS

PREFACE

It is important to note that throughout the reading, you will find *Quotes for Meditation* after each chapter. The quotes are drawn from men and women of different denominations, including those who devoted their lives to Christian theology and philosophy, and from Christian mystics and early church Roman Catholics. It is important to recognize that just because a quote has been added, it does not mean that I agree with everything they teach. The quotes are merely to encourage us to meditate more on Who God is and what He has done. The quotes vary in depth, but all of them should prove valuable in growing one's faith.

No one man or woman has all the answers. It is only the Word of God where the entirety of Truth can be found. The goal in collecting these quotes is to give you a widespread view of the perceptions of God by different denominations, theologians, and philosophers. Most quotes added are from sound Biblical teachers and preachers. A smaller number of quotes are from philosophers and Christian mystics who could see the One, True God, but whether they committed themselves fully to our Lord Jesus Christ is another matter.

I would like to additionally add that this book is not for the

Theologian or philosopher who seeks to argue or take positions of theological and philosophical debate. The purpose of this book is merely to draw others closer to God and give them a deeper understanding of Who the Trinitarian God is, what He has done, and how we should live our lives within the knowledge of His attributes.

Let us therefore enter what I hope to be an edifying read that will engage each of us in thinking more deeply about God. We can only know so much, but with the time we are given, we must make every effort to understand God as best we can. In understanding God better, we can face the trials and tribulations of this life with complete dependency, trust, and faith in Him.

Judah Veritas

Author

INTRODUCTION

"Our starting point must be the fact that God cannot be named... no mind has yet contained or language embraced God's substance in its fullness. No, we use facts connected with Him to outline qualities that correspond with Him, collecting a faint and feeble mental image from various quarters. Our noblest theologian is not one who has discovered the whole - our earthly shackles do not permit us the whole - but one whose mental image is by comparison fuller, who has gathered in his mind a richer picture, outline, or whatever we call it, of the truth."
— Gregory of Nazianzus

God's *Ineffable Attributes* have yet to be grasped and understood in full.

When we believe we have acquired an understanding of Who God is, we can rationally conclude that we have acquired just a touch of His splendor. One of the greatest words that can be used to describe God is "outside." God is both in and outside that which we can appropriately understand within our finite thinking. We may think He is, when in fact, He is beyond.

We may have words that describe Him that are true, but we cannot ascertain the validity that what we say is all there is. We may say God is holy with our own interpretation and understanding of the word, but there is much more behind each of His attributes that we are unaware of. This can be easily seen with each progressing revelation of God's attributes. As a born-again believer matures in this life, revelations of God continue to deepen and grow. With the words that we use and know, Scripture does aid us with clarity and understanding as to what these descriptive words entail. I do believe, however, that God was gracious enough to draw these words down to our level, in order that we might have the hope of understanding Who He is with our finite minds.

This life is but a warm-up to the eternal life that lies ahead. I believe that we will know more about God in the first ten minutes of eternity than we did in our entire lifetime on this earth. For though we walk by faith in this life, we will see our faith in full sight once in Heaven. We will see the entirety of our faith wrapped up in the precious face of our Lord Jesus Christ. Though we have the presence of God living within us as born-again believers, in Heaven, God's presence will be for all to see, all to hear, and all to experience without temptation, evil, and sin interrupting.

No matter our destination in the afterlife, we all will stand before the God of *Ineffable Attributes*. For the believer, all the emotions that humankind can experience will happen at once as we stand before Him. Though none of our friends or family will be able to advocate for us when our name is called to the Judgment Seat of Christ, we will have the One Advocate and the One Voice Who will present us to the Father and say, "This child is made righteous by My blood." By the blood of Christ, we are saved. By the Holy Spirit, we grow.

May Scriptural Truths and teachings wash over us as we grow in the Lord with each passing day.

Let us now go forward into what little justice can be done for such a holy, ineffable, incomprehensible God. May the Holy Spirit encourage each of us as we deepen our understanding of just how mighty and powerful our God is. May the appreciation of His *Ineffable Attributes* fuel the Holy Ghost fire of Truth, that we as genuine converts have nothing to fear. The problems of this life are fading and will be but a drop in the ocean of joy that is to come.

Heaven awaits our souls. God awaits His children. One day, we will all come to know God beyond comprehension. Once that point is reached, we will have just begun to know Him. Eternity cannot compete with our God, for His *Ineffable Attributes* transcend beyond it.

What a glorious, magnificent Truth awaits the born-again believer. How great it will be when our Jesus we shall see.

May all come to know the God of Abraham, Isaac, and Jacob.

* * *

*Heavenly Father, how great are You and how small we are. To meditate on the reality that You want a living relationship with us is beyond comprehension. What grace and love You have to be willing to place Your Spirit into broken vessels. Lord, we thank You for Your continued sanctifying work in the believer, and we thank You for the drawing of the Holy Spirit that led us to You. May we learn more about Your **Ineffable Attributes** with what little dialogue we have to speak, worship, and bring You praise. We want to understand You more, Father, so we ask for Your blessing upon us now. Show us Who You are through Your Word. Transcend our minds past surface-level faith. Grow us in knowledge, wisdom, and love, in order that we might bring You honor and glory, now and forevermore. In Jesus' name, Amen.*

HOLINESS

❦

WORTHY OF WORSHIP

*"*T*here is none holy like the Lord: for there is none besides You; there is no rock like our God."*
— *1 Samuel 2:2 ESV*

GOD'S HOLINESS illuminates both within Him and extends to those outside Him. His holiness transcends every good deed, good work, good word, and good act done by man. Combine all the "good" that man has done. Take everything "good" that both men and women have accomplished throughout all the ages of all time, and they will not compare to one drop of God Almighty's holiness! O, how holy is our Lord in Heaven! The magnitude of His holiness we cannot comprehend with our finite minds. How lost we become in His presence when we seek after His holiness. Let us open our ears, saints, to hear what is to be said of our holy God.

When we get to that Final Day and stand before the Lord, can you imagine what awe and wonder and beauty will be before us? The holiness of God will smite us down on our faces, prostrating before Him. On that day, what will we have to offer? Aside from the Holy Ghost

1

working in our lives, what did we do on our own that we can show God? Nothing but that which contradicts His nature and holiness.

Imagine seeing the white glow of His holiness blazing brighter than the sun. Though our eyes will be closed, and our faces will be towards the ground, His presence of white light will surround our entire being. If we tried to escape the light by shutting our eyelids, we would still see His holy light burn like a blazing fire. If we tried to appear calm before Him Who created all, we would possess a holy fear of Him all the more. His presence of holiness will be so powerful and inescapable, that we shall see and experience it whether we desire to or not. Remember "When Moses came down from Mount Sinai, with the two tablets of the testimony in his hand as he came down from the mountain, Moses did not know that the skin of his face shone because he had been talking with God" (Exodus 34:29 ESV). Can you see how our entire bodies will be surrounded by His glory and holiness? Who can stand? Who dares to believe that when we come face to face with God, we will simply go up and say, "Hey man, it's nice to finally meet you." Oh, no! Even the mightiest will fall flat on their faces. Even those who knew our Heavenly Father in the most intimate way will be in awe and in reverence before our Holy God.

Saints of God, see how the blessed John once laid his head upon the chest of Christ. See the brotherly affection they had. Christ said ""Truly, I say to you, among those born of women there has arisen no one greater than John the Baptist"" (Matthew 11:11 ESV). How great John the Baptist was esteemed because of his undying love for His Savior. Even John the Apostle spoke in Revelation 1:17 (NKJV), saying: "And when I saw Him, I fell at His feet as dead. But He laid His right hand on me, saying to me, "Do not be afraid; I am the First and the Last." O how we have lost the understanding of the holiness of God. How negligent we have been in understanding that God is in Heaven and we are on earth (Ecclesiastes 5:2). We are lower than the dust of the ground. What good can we bring apart from Him? O how wonderful it is to know who we are both apart from Christ and in Christ. Though the former produces humility, the latter produces a striving for holiness.

"For thus says the One who is high and lifted up, who inhabits eternity, whose name is Holy: "I dwell in the high and holy place, and also with him who is of a contrite and lowly spirit, to revive the spirit of the lowly, and to revive the heart of the contrite"" (Isaiah 57:15 ESV). See the indwelling of the Holy Spirit rest on us like a dove. Feel His presence. For the One Whose name is Holy dwells within our corrupt, broken temples. He comes to restore and renew our hearts and minds. Just as a mother and father seeks to clean their house before company comes, so the Holy Spirit seeks to clean and sanctify our temples before the return of Christ. How blessed we are to have the God, Who inhabits eternity, dwelling within us! O the blessed virtue of humility that sees how low man is before a Holy God. See how we are brought to a lowly and contrite heart when we view ourselves apart from Christ. How glorious it is, though, that God would send His Holy Spirit to reside in our being. We must know this miraculous truth and allow it to propel us forward down the path of righteousness. May we forever give praise to the One Who died for our sins and rose again, in order that we may die to ourselves and be raised again by the Holy Spirit.

Feel the refreshment of the soul as it meditates on the purity of God. The One without wrong or evil. The one Who is "of purer eyes than to behold evil, And cannot look on wickedness" (Habakkuk 1:13 NKJV). O, the great disgust and disdain of our sin and evil towards God! He is so holy that He cannot look upon our sin and wickedness without being enraged! Greater still, we must see the blessedness of our Lord and Savior, Jesus Christ, being our Mediator. See Him say to the Father, "I have died for this man and woman's sin. They are found in Me." Feel the warmth of God as He now says, ""For I will be merciful to their unrighteousness, and their sins and their lawless deeds I will remember no more"" (Hebrews 8:12 NKJV). O blessed Christ, the One and Only God-incarnated man Who walked this earth without blemish or stain of wrongdoing; blessed be His Holy Name. Blessed and holy is He to take on the weight of the world's sins. O, how the Lord does call all to Him through Christ's atoning sacrifice. May all come to know the loving-kindness that Christ revealed upon that Cross. For great is He Who is high and lifted up for all eternity!

What is our call then? What must we do with the wonderful gift of salvation? "I appeal to you therefore, brothers, by the mercies of God, to present your bodies as a living sacrifice, holy and acceptable to God, which is your spiritual worship" (Romans 12:1 ESV). We must live our life in a continual walk of sanctification; denying ourselves, taking up our Cross and following Christ (Matthew 16:24-26). We are called to lay down the world and take up the righteousness found through Christ's blood. We cannot be holy apart from the Holy Spirit. It is He that breathes upon us and reveals the way of holiness. He brings forth purity within our hearts. Our desires no longer stem from Adam, but from Christ. We are drawn forth by the Holy Spirit's direction. He leads us towards the One and Only Holy and Perfect God. He opens our minds to the realm which has no pain and no suffering; no sin and no evil. This blessed place of Heaven, which is simply the presence of Christ, is the place of eternal rest in Christ and worshiping of Christ. Let us see His arms open wide! Let us see the vision of us one day running towards our precious Savior to hug Him and fall before His feet in humility! O how this should drive us to be holy.

"Strive for peace with everyone, and for the holiness without which no one will see the Lord" (Hebrews 12:14 ESV). May the heart's desire of seeking after holiness set into motion the Undying Lamp that burns within. For we are the battalions of the Holy Ghost's flame! It is His holy fire that comes forth and can be seen by the external world. So long as we allow the Holy Spirit to come forth and present Himself to others, the transition of dying to the world and living for God is a fire with an undying kindle. No matter what it is; no matter how great or how small, the Holy Spirit can shine within us! His widespread fire touches those around us, drawing them to conviction of their sin and conversion through knowing Christ. We must remember that our lives are not the number of conversions we bring in. Our lives are the submission of what we allow the Holy Spirit to do. Nothing that is worth doing is done in our own strength. It is all done by the Holy Spirit. Holy is He!

"Oh sing to the LORD a new song, for He has done marvelous things! His right hand and His holy arm have worked salvation for him" (Psalm 98:1 ESV). How great and mighty are the creations of the heavenly realms. How majestic and powerful the cherubim and creatures of Heaven will be when our eyes gaze upon them! "And the four living creatures, each of them with six wings, are full of eyes all around and within, and day and night they never cease to say, "Holy, holy, holy, is the Lord God Almighty, Who was and is and is to come!"" (Revelation 4:8 ESV). Can you hear their songs echoing throughout all eternity? There will be no escape of the praise given to the high and Holy God. As we make our way throughout eternity, our hearts will be filled with God's holiness. Though we walk through the land in His holiness, we will all be individual images of God residing within His Presence. Our hearts will overflow with the holiness that can be forever felt and experienced.

The more we sing of His praises, the more jubilation we will have. Our feet will jump and dance! Our very desires and words will be lifted to the heights of the canvas of God's glory! Our hearts and minds will forever be focused upon Him! Our love for both each other and our precious Savior will never die. O how wonderful the constant indwelling of God will be both within and around us! There will be nothing to compete with; nothing to combat. To live for the Savior and worship Him will be the sole, simple desire of our inner being! For we are joint heirs and will rule and reign with Christ (Romans 8:17, 2 Timothy 2:12).

God's presence shall surround that blessed place of Heaven. For Heaven is simply the residing place of the holiness of Christ. Not even Heaven, however, will be able to contain the magnitude of our Heavenly Father's holiness. Though we are made holy by the Son, we ourselves will forever be growing and learning of the holiness of God. We will never be able to fully comprehend our Heavenly Father's holiness. His Holiness will never be understood in full. There will forever be something to learn about our Mighty God. We will forever gain a deeper revelation of Who our Father is. The joy that is to come should fill our spirits to strive and be holy just as He is Holy (1 Peter 1:15-16).

May we forever "Worship the LORD in the splendor of holiness" and "tremble before Him" (Psalm 96:9 ESV). God's holiness should not just bring us to awe and reverence, His holiness should make our hearts tremble at His Word. O how pitiful are the disputes of self-proclaimed Christians on this earth; bickering about God's Word and not believing what it says. We should tremble! It is the God of all time that has sustained The Scriptures and brought them into existence. These are the Words from God Almighty Himself. May we tremble at His Word and allow it to sink deep within our soul. May it keep us from seeking anything outside of holiness. May it be the Living Water within that brings forth life to our vessels. Let us always "Exalt the LORD our God; worship at His footstool! Holy is He!" (Psalm 99:5 ESV).

* * *

HEAVENLY FATHER, Your very name is Holy. Lord, our minds and hearts cannot comprehend the blessedness of such a God. One Who is pure and righteous in all His ways. Lord, a touch of Your holiness outweighs all the good that Your creation could complete on its own. Lord, we have no right for Your Holy Spirit to reside in us. Yet, we accept Him with everything in us. May He ignite the flame of holiness within our lives. May He lead us down the path of holiness. May He draw our minds to gaze upon Your holiness, trembling with all reverence and awe. O Lord, how the heavens shake at Your holiness. Who can compare to You, Almighty God? Not even the creatures of that heavenly place shall cease from singing "Holy, Holy, Holy is the Lord God Almighty". Forever they will live to give You praise. Lord, we thank You for being a God Who is pure and Holy and is willing to sanctify us into blessed saints of Your Kingdom. Holiness in our lives is all done by You and for You. We are not our own, Lord. Therefore, we come with open hearts that seek to surrender self and deny the desires of this flesh and this world, in order that we may be holy, just as You are Holy. In Jesus' name, Amen.

QUOTES FOR MEDITATION

1. "If you don't delight in the fact that your Father is holy, holy, holy, then you are spiritually dead. You may be in a church. You may go to a Christian school. But if there is no delight in your soul for the holiness of God, you don't know God. You don't love God. You're out of touch with God. You're asleep to His character." **R.C. Sproul**

2. "It is an undoubted truth that every doctrine that comes from God, leads to God; and that which doth not tend to promote holiness is not of God." **George Whitefield**

3. "Anything that belittles or obliterates the holiness of God by a false view of the love of God, is untrue to the revelation of God given by Jesus Christ." **Oswald Chambers**

4. "The holiness of God teaches us that there is only one way to deal with sin- radically, seriously, painfully, constantly. If you do not so live, you do not live in the presence of the Holy One of Israel." **Sinclair B. Ferguson**

5. "We know nothing like the Divine holiness. It stands apart, unique, unapproachable, incomprehensible and unattainable. The natural man is blind to it. He may fear

God's power and admire His wisdom, but His holiness he cannot even imagine." **A.W. Tozer**

IMMANENCE

INDWELLING IN ALL THINGS

"Am I a God at hand, declares the Lord, and not a God far away?""
— *Jeremiah 23:23 ESV*

OUR GOD DWELLS within both time and the universe. Not only does He exist in it; He is outside it. Though He be far, He is near. When we become born-again believers, the very presence of God lives within us. We may shout at the mountain top, and He hears us from the clouds. We may pray within our heads, and He is there, listening. There is not a place where God is not, for the very word "place" is and belongs to God. God is "place". He exists and moves everywhere. There is nothing outside His reach. "Where shall I go from Your Spirit? Or where shall I flee from Your presence? If I ascend to heaven, You are there! If I make my bed in Sheol, You are there! If I take the wings of the morning and dwell in the uttermost parts of the sea, even there Your hand shall lead me, and Your right hand shall hold me. If I say, "Surely the darkness shall cover me, and the light about me be night," even the darkness is not dark to You; the night is bright as the day, for darkness is as light with You" (Psalm 139:7-12 ESV).

See the cloud that moves across the sky, God dwells within it. See the grass that sways in the wind, God dwells within it. See the horse gallop across the prairie, God dwells within it. See a group where two or more are gathered together, God dwells within them (Matthew 18:20). See the birds soar across the sky in calm flight, God dwells within them. See the earth orbit the sun, God dwells within it. See the stars shine ever so bright at the dusk of night, God dwells within them. See the galaxies of the Universe, God dwells within them. There is no place where God is not, for His Presence and Power is within that which He has created. God is not only within that which He has created, His presence transcends beyond it.

To push it a step further beyond God's immanence of His physical creation, God also dwells within our good works and deeds that are done by the Holy Spirit. When actions and speech proceed from the presence of the Holy Spirit, they are done in the airwaves where God dwells. When our hands move to lift a heavy object for someone who needs help, God dwells within that very act of motion. He is not only in the object, but He is in us. God is not only in us, but He is in the very act itself. The realm in which the act is done, there God dwells doing it for His glory. Likewise, when words of encouragement and conviction come forth in Truth, God dwells within the wavelengths of what is said.

Though God dwells within our very breath (for our breath alone comes from Him), so a believer's words bring Him glory. God dwells within the very words that come forth in Truth, and He exists in the realm in which those words will proceed and be heard. Just as God awaits Himself in the future (though He already dwells there), God awaits Truth that is uttered from our lips, even though He is already living inside us and is the Truth.

Great is the mystery of the future within our lives. For God has already been to our future. For not only does God dwell within time, but time dwells with God. Like a recorded game that can be played and reviewed, so our lives are before God. He holds the recording of our life in His hands; yet, He watches it in the present. Though He already knows what the end of the recording is, He chooses to see, walk, and be with us in our present. When we hurt, He is there. When we love, He is there. When we are frightened, He brings comfort. When we are distressed, He brings peace. No matter what comes in this life, God already knows. Therefore, His preparations are already set. All we must do is seek Him in the midst of calamity and prosperity. "In the day of prosperity be joyful, and in the day of adversity consider: God has made the one as well as the other, so that man may not find out anything that will be after him" (Ecclesiastes 7:14 ESV).

Not only has God been to the future, He is the future. What awaits beyond, no man or spirit can comprehend but God alone. "A man's heart plans his way, But the LORD directs his steps" (Proverbs 16:9 NKJV). We may believe that our future will look a certain way, but it is the God of time that holds our future. The enemy may try to deplete and destroy a godly, active, spiritual relationship with the Father, but He can do nothing more than bring temptation (unless the Lord permits otherwise). No being, no situation, no circumstance, and no person can operate outside of God's immanence. God is already there waiting to do what He has already decided needs to be done. God rules perfectly because He knows perfectly. To have forever existed in the eternal past, while at the same time living in both the present and the future brings validity and confirmation that there is nothing our God cannot fix or do that does not have His immanence in it.

"And He made from one man every nation of mankind to live on all the face of the earth, having determined allotted periods and the boundaries of their dwelling place, that they should seek God, and perhaps feel their way toward him and find him. Yet He is actually not far from each one of us, for "'In Him we live and move and have our being'; as even some of your own poets have said, "'For we are indeed His offspring'" (Acts 17:26-28 ESV). Though God be *outside* time and outside space, He is also *in* time and in space. Aside from sin and evil, there is nothing that is without God being within. If God *made* all and is *outside* all, then His Presence *is in* all. We live and move and have our being in Him. We have breath in our lungs because of Him. Our hearts beat to the rhythm of His immanence. Everything operates within the realm of God. There is nothing hidden. Nothing goes unseen. Though man may not see, God does see. He is beside us, behind us, in front of us, and, for the believer, in us. Though man does not see our every step, God does.

"The Spirit of God has made me, and the breath of the Almighty gives me life" (Job 33:4). God is more present than the air in which we breathe because He is the Creator of breath itself. Just as He is everywhere, He is also in everything. From the largest spectacle to the smallest atom, God's immanence can be found there. Though His immanence is within all, He is not dictated or confined by time and space. For God simply cannot, not be. Whatever our eyes gaze upon, He is there, but not solely. God is collectively within His creation. He is immanently involved in the sum of all time, space, matter, and energy, while remaining entirely beyond it all. When we worship and praise God, we do not worship and praise a tree, nor do we worship and praise the sky. His beauty is simply made known through what He has created. His immanence is seen in His creation, but His immanence is not bound by His creation. For to create, one must be outside that which they create. Just as a woodworker builds a beautiful table, he himself must be outside the supplies to create what he has envisioned within his mind. Likewise, God has always envisioned from eternity past the creation in which we see. God's Being had to have existed outside that which He created, otherwise He would not be the God of immanence.

"If He should set His heart to it and gather to Himself His Spirit and His breath, all flesh would perish together, and man would return to dust" (Job 34:14-15 ESV). As God dwells within all, we cannot dwell on this earth without God. If He were to gather all of Himself, by Himself, for Himself, we would immediately dwindle away. We cannot live without His presence. God must be there in order that we may live. God must be present if we are to survive. Even though many men live their lives *apart* from God, mankind cannot walk on this earth and live *without* God. For man, it takes God to reject God. Man cannot live without God. However, as man lives in God's *being*, man can choose to reject God's *presence* with his libertarian free-will decision. Though God is everywhere, man can reject God's longsuffering patience. So much so, that a man is finally given over to a conscience that believes God is not there, even though God in fact is.

Let us remember that God is ever-present. He dwells within and outside everything. He has created all and is above all. Everything that is, lies within God Himself. We cannot live a life that wallows in depression and hopelessness when we know that God is immanent. As long as we are breathing, God is calling. Will we listen to our immanent God so that we may walk into His promises and purpose for our lives? The future will involve strife, trial, and tribulation, but our God promises to be there every step of the way. The person that holds fast to Christ and, by the power of the Holy Spirit, endures for Him will have a life that will forever be enriched by the glorious joy and peace of God's immanence. His immanence will bring forth indescribable ecstasy and jubilation once we have been covered by the Blood and we have received the promised hope of an eternity in Heaven. May we forever know that "The LORD is near to all who call on Him, to all who call on Him in truth" (Psalm 145:18 ESV).

* * *

O IMMANENT FATHER, we come before You with great wonder of Your indwelling presence within our lives. Your very Being is beyond comprehension. Yet, we receive what we can know about You with all joy and awe. You truly are an amazing God. Lord, may the truth of Your immanence take place within our soul. May we walk throughout all the days of our lives in perfect peace, knowing that You are with us. Though You surround us, God, You are in us. We thank You for the Holy Spirit Who presents Truth to us. Lord, may we bring honor and glory to You every second of every day, for You are worthy of praise. In Jesus' name, Amen.

QUOTES FOR MEDITATION

1. "What now does the divine immanence mean in direct Christian experience? It means simply that God is here. Wherever we are, God is here. There is no place, there can be no place, where He is not." **A.W. Tozer**
2. "Such an emphasis on the immanence of God as Creator in, with, and under the natural processes of the world unveiled by the sciences is certainly in accord with all that the sciences have revealed since those debates of the nineteenth century." **Arthur Peacocke**
3. "Christianity is the only religion in the world where a man's God comes and lives inside of him!" **Leonard Ravenhill**
4. "God dwells in eternity but time dwells in God. He has already lived all our tomorrows as He has lived all our yesterdays." **A.W. Tozer**
5. "O Supreme and Unapproachable Light! O Whole and Blessed Truth, how far art Thou from me, who am so near to Thee! How far removed art Thou from my vision, though I am so near to Thine! Everywhere Thou art wholly present, and I see Thee not. In Thee I move, and in Thee I have my

being; and I cannot come to Thee. Thou art within me, and about me, and I feel Thee not." **Anselm of Canterbury**

IMMENSITY

THE QUALITY OR STATE OF BEING IMMENSE

"*Thus says the LORD: "Heaven is My throne, and the earth is My footstool; what is the house that you would build for Me, and what is the place of My rest?"*"
— *Isaiah 66:1 ESV*

MANY FALSE GODS ARE MAN-MADE. They are physical, man-made constructions that must be carried from place to place. The God of Abraham, Isaac, and Jacob, however, is beyond the physical realm. The immensity of our Lord Jesus Christ can be seen throughout creation and the Scriptures. "Heaven is My throne, and the earth is My footstool" describes God's immensity, for He Himself cannot be contained. "In His hand are the depths of the earth, and the mountain peaks belong to Him" (Psalm 95:4 NIV).

We are but ants walking amid God's presence. Yet, He chooses to have a living relationship with us. The God Who sees the entire world in one glance, sees us. He is nearer than our very heartbeat. At the same time, He holds earth in the palm of His hand. How great and mighty is God! Though He is more powerful than all, He brings Himself down to all. He is worthy of worship whether He is seen in the butterfly that floats across the grass, or through the stars that shine at night. No matter what we see, He is there. Even when the eyes of a born-again believer close for rest, He can be found within us, speaking and residing in our temples.

What a beautiful passage Isaiah 40:12-15 (ESV) displays of God's immensity:

"Who has measured the waters in the hollow of His hand and marked off the heavens with a span, enclosed the dust of the earth in a measure and weighed the mountains in scales and the hills in a balance? Who has measured the Spirit of the LORD, or what man shows Him His counsel? Whom did He consult, and who made Him understand? Who taught Him the path of justice, and taught Him knowledge, and showed Him the way of understanding? Behold, the nations are like a drop from a bucket, and are accounted as the dust on the scales; behold, He takes up the coastlands like fine dust."

O the beauty of God and the illuminating light that is displayed through His majesty! Who made our Heavenly Father understand wisdom? Who perfected the landscape of the earth? Who gave every-thing purpose? Who understands the meaning behind every living thing? Who is the One Who can see all? Only God Almighty. No one is greater, no one is higher, no one knows all like our Lord Jesus Christ. He is Thee Colossal of all colossal. His glory outshines any ray of the sun! His immensity has no bounds. There is nothing that can contain God, for only God contains Himself. Nothing that lies within Him can go outside Him.

O the glorious truth to understand that nothing can outdo our God. Two-thousand demons could not stand against one spoken word from our Lord Jesus Christ (Mark 5)! Though man be ignorant and foolish with their scoffing and Atheistic practices, the demons have a clear understanding of our Heavenly Father. "Even the demons believe—and shudder!" (James 2:19 ESV). The demons quake and tremble at the immensity of God. How fearful they are. They are but ants ready to be trampled on by Christ's foot. They are but flies amid His presence. Demons lack all authority when they stand in the pres-ence of the One Who died and rose again on the third day. What do we as believers have to fear? The great immensity of our God cannot be fought, bought, or attained. Though many may envy His power and authority, none can take it. God will forever rule and reign as the most immense Being. Not even time and space can hold Him, for they reside within Him.

""Am I a God at hand, declares the LORD, and not a God far away? Can a man hide himself in secret places so that I cannot see him? declares the LORD. Do I not fill heaven and earth?" declares the LORD" (Jeremiah 23:23-24 ESV). God's immensity allows Him to see all. There is no place that man can hide himself where God is not. To believe that man can go to the darkest cave and do as he please without being seen is to believe that one can run the track of an Olympic game and not be spotted. The eyes of God are ever present. They flow through time, space, and matter. The world and the universe sit within the eye of God. There is nowhere that God is not. His immensity overrides human understanding.

Only by God and through God do all things exist. "The God Who made the world and everything in it, being Lord of heaven and earth, does not live in temples made by man, nor is He served by human hands, as though He needed anything, since He Himself gives to all mankind life and breath and everything" (Acts 17:24 ESV). God cannot be served, for He already serves Himself through our vessels, when the Holy Spirit resides. We cannot do anything worthwhile without His doing. We cannot give anything to God that He does not already possess. God has already constructed the very best for our lives. We must simply have a heart that seeks it out by seeking Him.

The deepest and most grandeur things belong to the Maker and Ruler of all: ""Can you find out the deep things of God? Can you find out the limit of the Almighty? It is higher than heaven—what can you do? Deeper than Sheol—what can you know? Its measure is longer than the earth and broader than the sea" (Job 11:7-9 ESV). If God is higher than the heavens; if He extends further than the east is from the west; if He can magnify Himself in all atoms and molecules, then we can trust in His immensity. We can believe that God is not only unconquerable, but incomparable. Just as a child could not stand against the greatest boxer in the world, so nothing can stand against God. Likewise, just as the greatest boxer would not harm a child, so God's immense love does not seek to destroy us. His love desires to save.

God's love transcends human comprehension. It is whom society marginalizes, that God calls. Who we would call the most wretched human beings to walk this earth, God sees as projects to be loved and drawn to Him. Who we would deem as the lowest worm of the earth, God sees as an opportunity to make a living testimony. There is no greater love than the love of Christ. He bore our punishment upon that Cross. Christ died for all of mankind's sins. How immense the love of the Father was to turn a blind eye towards His Son. How immense the love of God was for us to have the Father turn from His Son's cry, "Eli, Eli, lema sabachthani?" that is, "My God, My God, why have You forsaken Me?"" (Matthew 27:46). How it grieved and hurt the Father's heart to turn away. O how blessed is man to have the opportunity to have a living relationship and partake in fellowship with such a God! A God of immense love! Immense grace! Immense mercy!

We do not deserve such a blessed gift as our Savior's crucifixion. How precious each drop was. More than all of mankind's good deeds could not compare to one drop of Christ's blood! How precious He is to our hearts and our minds. How soothing this immense love is to the soul as the Holy Spirit rests upon us. Sweet Jesus, how great and immense Your humility was and is! O Heavenly Father, how immense Your endearment and tenderness towards Your creation was and is! O Holy Spirit, how immense is Your warmth and intimacy with those who belong to Christ.

Though we speak about such beauty, we are not worthy of understanding God's love. How pure His immensity is that though He be above all, He cares for all. How great a truth that not only does He care for all, He sees all. Thank You, Father, for being above all and seeing all things. ""If they dig into Sheol, from there shall My hand take them; if they climb up to heaven, from there I will bring them down. If they hide themselves on the top of Carmel, from there I will search them out and take them; and if they hide from My sight at the bottom of the sea, there I will command the serpent, and it shall bite them"" (Amos 9:2-3 ESV). No evil escapes God's sight. No good done by the Holy Ghost goes unnoticed. There is no escape from God's immensity.

May we allow this Truth to flow through our being. May we know that as long as we are alive as believers, we have nothing to fear, for God is near.

* * *

HEAVENLY FATHER, we come before You with all humility. O God, how great is Your love that You were willing to have Your Son die for the sins of mankind. Despite the ungodly, wicked mockery and persecution Your Son went through, You remained longsuffering on Hell-bent people. Lord, we have ruined all good that You have designed, but O how blessed is the promise of a new heaven and a new earth for the believer. God, we rest in Your immensity. We take pleasure in knowing that demons shudder at the name of Christ. We are not worthy to be on Christ's side of eternity, but we accept it with all humility. Lord, may we walk boldly before mankind, knowing that You see all and are outside all. We have nothing to fear when Your loving arms wrap around our souls. O Heavenly Father, how grateful we are for Your immensity. In Jesus' name, Amen.

QUOTES FOR MEDITATION

1. "God's love fills the immensity of space; therefore, there is no shortage of love in the universe, only in our willingness to do what is needed to feel it." **John H. Groberg**
2. "Christ is the aperture through which the immensity and magnificence of God can be seen." **John Bertram Phillips**
3. "God is as great in minuteness as He is in magnitude." **Charles Caleb Colton**
4. "Whence it follows that God is absolutely perfect, since perfection is nothing but magnitude of positive reality, in the strict sense, setting aside the limits or bounds in things which are limited." **Gottfried Leibniz**

INFINITUDE

THE QUALITY OR STATE OF BEING INFINITE

"*The Lord is high above all nations, and His glory above the heavens! Who is like the Lord our God, Who is seated on high, Who looks far down on the heavens and the earth?*"
— *Psalm 113:4-6 ESV*

ATTEMPT TO WEIGH GOD, and you will find He weighs nothing. Yet, at the same time, He weighs everything. Try and measure the width of our awesome God. He extends further than the East is from the West. Test His ability to go beyond the furthest star and it will be like taking one step here on earth for Him. Who can constrict our God? He is the Alpha and Omega. Nothing can contain Him. Nothing can hold Him. Nothing can constrain Him. No presence, power, or might can extinguish His infinitude. All the powers of this world and all the physicality of the universe are but a grain of sand compared to Him.

For sake of comprehension, let us imagine that both the universe and everything contained within the universe is represented as a grain of sand. Now, let us imagine the sun as a representation of God. Try to set that grain of sand next to the sun and see how it becomes incinerated within an instant. Look at the size compared to the sun. See how small that grain of sand is to the burning ball of fire we call the sun. Though the grain of sand is something, it is impossible to see that single spec when viewing the entirety of the sun. Likewise, is God's infinitude. To be able to have a mind that can comprehend and grasp the entirety of His infinitude would be to not see ourselves, the earth, the galaxies, or even the universe in the process. Just as the grain of sand cannot be seen in a picture where it sits next to the sun, so the universe cannot be seen when measured and compared to the infinitude of Almighty God.

It is easier to look for a moving ant on top of the largest mountain, than it is to comprehend the fullness of the infinitude of God. No human being of such finite, limited thinking can sit upon the vast greatness of our God. How limited we are in the sight of a limitless God. Who walks upon this earth that can fly without assistance? Yet, God needs no flight. His infinitude is so vast that wherever "there" be, He is already there. Though it takes millions and billions of years for man to reach the nearest star, God is there within less than a second. For the distance from Earth to the nearest star is God Himself. "And He is before all things, and in Him all things hold together" (Colossians 1:17 ESV).

O how marvelous is the vastness of God's infinitude. There is no word for extension, for wherever that place of extension is, God is there. No eye can see past, no mind can think beyond, no atom can extend further to a place where God is not already. How wonderful and splendid is this truth. Who can attempt to understand such a boundless Being? Who dares try to pass the never-ending Being Who is the ""Alpha and the Omega...Who is and Who was and Who is to come, the Almighty"" (Revelation 1:8 ESV)? O how every knee should bow before such a God of cosmic magnitude. How we all should be in reverence and awe of the God Who is unsearchable. Though He lies within the born-again believer, He is not the born-again believer. Though God is in the water that rushes forth in the ocean, He is not the ocean. Though God is in the galaxies we see, He is not the galaxies. All of these are but little pebbles in His hands. Since God is able to make something out of nothing, then surely, He can make that which He has created be but the size of an atom compared to His infinite Being.

Imagine, the universe is a picture. Greater than this, imagine that Heaven is a picture outside the picture of the universe. Again, imagine that God is a picture outside the picture of Heaven. Since God is Infinite, imagine a picture of God being outside a picture of God, being a picture outside of God, etc. Multiply this process one-hundred-fold. Once we have reached this perpetual motion of God's infinitude being a picture, within a picture, within a picture (for one-hundred consecutive times), our understanding of God's infinitude will be like reading one word out of the whole Bible. Do we dare transcend further into an understanding so complex and so vast, that our very minds would burst in awe and wonder of how such an Infinite Being could see each one of us? How great is His size not only in Being, but in character.

Though God is interminable, He brings His focus down upon us, His creation. Those made in His image He calls to know Him. Those who know Him, He resides in them. How miraculous is it that the God of this universe resides within the genuine, converted Christian! Who can comprehend what power and what magnitude lies within? Not power to be used for harm, but to further God's Kingdom. The power to love in the midst of hatred. The power to forgive in the midst of a heinous act. The power of grace in the face of human depravity. The power to be kind towards the most ruthless of men. Dear brother and sister, "Great is the LORD, and greatly to be praised, and His greatness is unsearchable" (Psalm 145:3 ESV).

What greatness lies within us. Not because we are great, but because of God's very Spirit. We have God in us. God in us! The God of infinitude Whose greatness is unsearchable can be found within us. Though He is in us, He is still unsearchable. Though the Holy Spirit be an intimate friend to those Who seek His will and His presence, we still lack the appropriate comprehension of Who He actually is. We cannot begin to understand the complexity of a Spirit within our spirit. We cannot understand that God has stamped the Cross of Christ upon our hearts and has made us forever His. How great is this wonderment! It should propel us towards searching after the unsearchable God. Though we will never fully comprehend Him all throughout eternity in Heaven, He allows us to grow little by little with understanding the un-understandable. He allows us to see the unseeable. Through the spiritual life that is derived from an intimate connection with our Lord and Savior, Jesus Christ, we can experience the presence of One Who is beyond comprehension.

How this should motivate us to press into the God of infinitude. How this should excite the soul to be ruled by our never-ending God. The Colossal God Who looks upon even the deadliest, deafening problems of our day and can cast them outside our very galaxy. His infinitude allows Him the ability to descend and come into each problem of our day and operate within the realm of our situations. He does so with effortless strength and perfect omniscience. For God can be within every situation of every person and act accordingly at any given time. We must simply rest in His infinitude and seek His face and pray that His limitless hand would move upon our lives.

* * *

HEAVENLY FATHER, how large and vast You are. Your ways are unsearchable. Your Being transcends understanding. All of Heaven cannot contain You. All of eternity cannot comprehend You. How great You are, Lord, to be willing to see us in the midst of this world. How small we are in Your sight. Yet, how You loved us enough to send Your Son to die upon the Cross for our sins. We give You praise for such an act. Lord, the very blood of Christ that dripped down upon that Cross showed the infinitude of love that You have for Your creation. It is the act of Your infinite love that will be echoed throughout all eternity. For it is by Christ's precious blood we live. So long as Christ lives, Heaven is our home. What a glorious revelation to behold such love You have for us, O God of infinitude. We thank You, Father, for being bigger than all creation and all our problems. May our hearts rest in the Truth that You see all because You are beyond all. We give You all the praise and glory, O God of Infinitude. In Jesus' name, Amen.

QUOTES FOR MEDITATION

1. "In God there is an infinitude of things which I cannot comprehend, nor possibly even reach in any way by thought; for it is the nature of the infinite that my nature, which is finite and limited, should not comprehend it."
   Rene Descartes
2. "We come no nearer the infinitude of the creative power of God, if we enclose the space of its revelation within a sphere described with the radius of the Milky Way, then if we were to limit it to a ball an inch in diameter. All that is finite, whatever has limits and a definite relation to unity, is equally far removed from the infinite... Eternity is not sufficient to embrace the manifestations of the Supreme Being, if it is not combined with the infinitude of space."
   Immanuel Kant
3. "We know that there is an infinite, and we know not its nature. As we know it to be false that numbers are finite, it is therefore true that there is a numerical infinity. But we know not of what kind; it is untrue that it is even, untrue that it is odd; for the addition of a unit does not change its nature; yet it is a number, and every number is odd or even

(this certainly holds of every finite number). Thus we may quite well know that there is a God without knowing what He is." **Blaise Pascal**

4. "We never have a full demonstration, although there is always an underlying reason for the truth, even if it is only perfectly understood by God, who alone penetrated the infinite series in one stroke of the mind." **Gottfried Leibniz**

5. "We know then the existence and nature of the finite, because we also are finite and have extension. We know the existence of the infinite and are ignorant of its nature, because it has extension like us, but not limits like us. But we know neither the existence nor the nature of God, because he has neither extension nor limits." **Blaise Pascal**

OMNIPRESENT

❧

PRESENT EVERYWHERE ALWAYS

"*The eyes of the Lord are in every place, keeping watch on the evil and the good.*"
— **Proverbs 15:3 ESV**

As everything comes from God, so God sees everything which comes from Him. There is nothing that escapes His eye. Everything that is done in private, is done in public when done before our Holy God. He sees all. Try and whisper a word of gossip within the deepest cave of earth. God hears it as if we shouted it through a megaphone in a church service. No matter what we do, what we say, or what we think, God is there.

God resides in the deepest parts of the earth. There is nothing too deep that can hide from Him and nothing too far that is beyond Him. God is forever present. God is always "there". If we are talking with friends, it is as if He is listening as another person within the conversation. If we are on top of a mountain, He sees us from every angle. Though we speak from a place where man cannot hear us, God is there listening. No one can say, think, or act where God is not. Just as a little girl has her doll house and sees everything within the house, so

God views all His creation in the same manner. If God created it, we can be sure He is there watching everything that takes place.

God is not only present in the physical realm, but also in the metaphysical realm. His omnipresence is so vast and so beyond comprehension, that He is also present within the mind. When we are convicted, that is God drawing us towards Truth. When a born-again believer hears a voice that speaks Truth and provides counsel and guidance, we can rest assured that it is God Who speaks. As our thoughts roam within the foundation of our being, God is present there. There is no place where God is not listening, watching, hearing, and seeing everything that is done and said. The omnipresence of God Almighty may scare many, but it is a comfort to those who desire to distance themselves from sin and seek God's will.

God in His omnipresence is able to detect and see what must be done to further His Kingdom. "I will instruct you and teach you in the way you should go; I will counsel you with My eye upon you" (Psalm 32:8 ESV). We can trust that because God is able to see all He is able to direct us in the best possible way. This direction floods us with grace and Truth. It gives us the confidence to know that He will direct us to the right people, the right conversations, the right thoughts, and the right situations in which the Holy Spirit can fulfill His will within our lives. Since everything lies before God's eye, we can also know that we are protected by Him. His omnipresence leads into His omnicompetence. God is able to do what is right and just based upon what He sees going on within a person, a particular situation, and the world. His omnipresence should bring peace to the soul. It should draw us out of our situation and bring us forth into the heavenly realms of perfect peace in our Heavenly Father. Who can do wrong without consequence when God Almighty sees all?

O how the blessed truth of God's omnipresence ought to comfort our lives. To know God is there and that He will be there through our trials, tribulations, successes, and blessings. There is nothing in this life that we will go through that God does not see and is not present. This truth should rest our hurried spirits to know that God is there to guide us along in this life. ""No one will be able to stand against you all the days of your life. As I was with Moses, so I will be with you; I will never leave you nor forsake you"" (Joshua 1:5 NIV).

We have nothing to fear when we have Christ's Cross stamped on our soul. God will neither leave us nor forsake us. We are promised that the God of all will be with us through all. If we need comfort, we can call on the Comforter. If we need advice, we can ask the Advocate. If we need help, we can call upon the Helper. Why is this possible? All because of belief in Christ and His atoning sacrifice. We not only have God as a spectator of our lives, but He becomes the Life of our lives Who dwells within. Perfect, pure, righteous, and holy is He, that dwells within our broken vessels. This is Who we know to be the Holy Spirit, and it is only the Holy Spirit Who can bring healing and comfort to our brokenness. It is He that makes God's omnipresence real to us.

Knowing that God is ever-present helps us to be honest with ourselves. It should propel us to seek and search out what truly lies within us. If God is omnipresent, then we cannot fool Him. If He sees all, then He knows all. We cannot lie to Him like we do to a friend or family member and expect Him not to know. "You search out my path and my lying down and are acquainted with all my ways" (Psalm 139:3 ESV). God is there when we work, when we sleep, when we socialize, when we are in public, and when we are in private. Just as a boss may shadow his worker for a few days to make sure they are doing their work appropriately, so God shadows us every day seeing how we act and correspond with the realities of life. God knows us better than we know ourselves because He sees outside ourselves when viewing how we speak, act, and think. Though He is present within not just the body and soul of a born-again believer, He is also outside, watching how we walk. If danger lies ahead and His perfect will says it is not time for us to come Home, God will work through His omnipotence and omniscience to direct us away from harm. He will move us towards that which will keep us safe as we continue sharing the Gospel and being a living testimony for Him. We can trust in the truth that His omnipresence will forever guide, lead, and bring comfort to us.

When someone is present somewhere, they cannot be present somewhere else. It is impossible to capture someone in Europe when they are living in the United States. God, however, is omnipresent within the entirety of the earth's matter. God moves and is not only in the matter, but within the air. Not only is God within the air, but He is also in the realm of thoughts. Not only is He in our thoughts, but His presence also extends into the universe. Not only is God in the universe, but He is also outside it. One cannot create something without being outside it. Likewise, God is outside all He creates. Though we may create something, we cannot be in it. God, however, can be in what He creates because He is not a physical being. Though Jesus Christ was the God-incarnate man, God Himself cannot be seen *fully*. God can be seen everywhere and at different points, but no one is able to see God *entirely*. God is not confined by space and matter. Therefore, His presence extends beyond space and matter.

"Thus says the LORD: "Heaven is my throne, and the earth is My footstool; what is the house that you would build for Me, and what is the place of My rest?" (Isaiah 66:1 ESV). No one will ever be able to bring God fully to one centralized location unless that centralized location be God Himself. This would extend beyond human reasoning and comprehension. For God centralized is all we see and know, yet it is also beyond all we see and know. God can be seen anywhere because He is everywhere. *However, God cannot be solely and fully in one thing at one given time; for if that could be possible within our given realm, He would not be God.* To believe all of God can be brought into a mountain would dissolve His omnipresence. God has revealed the knowledge of His Being in such a way where all of what we see resides within Him. Still, whatever cannot be seen or cannot be comprehended is within God because God oversees all. There is no idea or realm in which God is not.

To try and escape God's presence is just as good as trying to hold the moon on one's back. One cannot run from God. This truth should propel the unbeliever to fear God and come to know Him. This truth should speak to the born-again believer and give assurance that God is there to comfort and aid us. We do not have a God Who comes and goes. Rather, we have a God Who is there. For wherever "there" is, there one can find God Almighty.

* * *

ALMIGHTY GOD, how grateful we are for Your eternal and everlasting presence. Lord, what peace comes in knowing that wherever we are, You are there. Lord, You see all and hear all. We are thankful to know You, Father. We are thankful for Your omnipresence. Who can run or escape from You? Since You see all, O God, we can trust that You will always do what is right. How comforting it is to know You, God. No one can surpass You, for You are the Omnipresent One. Rule our minds, O Lord. Be not only omnipresent within our being and our thoughts but have Your way in us. We seek not to suppress or grieve You, Holy Spirit. We want to forever have Your omnipresence be in us, but also flowing through us. May Your presence be what guides us to do what is right. May Your thoughts of wisdom, love and discernment be forever present within our hearts and minds. We long to glorify You, Lord. Be God not only to us, but through us. May we be vessels in which the Holy Spirit works in a mighty way for Your Kingdom. In Jesus' name, Amen.

QUOTES FOR MEDITATION

1. "The eternal silence of these infinite spaces frightens me." **Blaise Pascal**
2. "Let us quake before the great Spirit, Who is my God, Who has made me know God, Who is God there above, and Who forms God here: almighty, imparting manifold gifts, Him Whom the holy choir hymns, Who brings life to those in heaven and on earth, and is enthroned on high, coming from the Father, the Divine force, self-commandeered; He is not a Child (for there is one worthy Child of the One who is best), nor is He outside the unseen Godhead, but of identical honor." **Gregory of Nazianzus**
3. "When men search for God with their bodily eyes they find Him nowhere, for He is invisible. But for those who ponder in the Spirit He is present everywhere. He is in all, yet beyond all." **Symeon the New Theologian**
4. "The Scriptures teach that God is infinite. This means that His being knows no limits. Therefore there can be no limit to His presence; He is omnipresent. In His infinitude He surrounds the finite creation and contains it." **A.W. Tozer**

5. "God is indeed there. He is there as He is here and everywhere, not confined to tree or stone, but free in the universe, near to everything, next to everyone, and through Jesus Christ immediately accessible to every loving heart. The doctrine of the Divine omnipresence decides this forever." **A.W. Tozer**

OMNIBENEVOLENT

❧

POSSESSING PERFECT OR
UNLIMITED GOODNESS

"*or the Lord is good; His mercy is everlasting, And His truth endures to all generations.*"
— *Psalm 100:5 NKJV*

MANY OF GOD'S attributes can be found within His omnibenevolence. God's omnibenevolence is not simply unlimited goodness. It is also what ties into it that helps us grasp the reality of how good God is. Grace, mercy, love, and truth are all found within God and His unlimited goodness. None of these are out of balance, but all flow through the same, perfect stream from God Himself. The Lord is Good. He is far more merciful and gracious than we could understand. As He brought us out of what we once were involved with in the past, He continues to sanctify us by His Holy Spirit to distance us from sin and draw us closer to Him. Through His omnibenevolence towards mankind, He is longsuffering and wanting all to come to know Him (2 Peter 3:9).

How can we see drunkards, idolaters, fornicators, drug-addicts, swindlers, adulterers, and the sexually immoral and not believe that

God is longsuffering? His goodness through patience endures beyond what we could ever fathom. Who would allow someone to use their mother or father's name in vain and curse them? Who would tolerate their son being mocked, scoffed at, and ridiculed? Yet, God, in His omnibenevolence, is longsuffering. Our Holy God tolerates sin for a finite time. This finite time is long-lasting. If it were not, we *all* would be damned.

Think about your past: what is it that you were involved in for so long? What ruled your body, your mind, and your heart? Was it envy? Pride? Ego? Was it self-pleasure or self-fulfillment? God in His unlimited goodness understands that He must be longsuffering if any of us are to make it to the Cross of Christ and repent. He does not *approve,* but rather *allows* us to sin – based upon our libertarian free will – to show us that there is no fulfillment and satisfaction in the things of the flesh and the world. God's omnibenevolence is calling all of us out of our wretched lifestyles of sin that are found in the root of Adam. He is calling us all to Him. Let us "Seek the Lord while He may be found, Call upon Him while He is near" (Isaiah 55:6 NKJV).

Before we are called to the other side of eternity, God's omnibenevolence offers each and every person the ability to accept or reject Truth. As we know from Romans 1:20, all have a general revelation of knowing that there is a God. None will be able to show up on Judgment Day with an excuse. Though some have never heard the Gospel presented or heard the name of Jesus Christ, they will have been given equal opportunity through the drawing and conviction of the Holy Spirit that there is a God. Likewise, God will forever be calling and drawing our hearts to the Truth – whether through His Word or general revelation – by the working of His Holy Spirit upon our lives. As 2 Peter 3:9 reveals, God wants none to perish. In His omnibenevolence, He continues to work on drawing us towards Him until the time we pass into eternity.

We can believe and trust that if someone presents the Gospel in a distorted, perverted fashion (Such as I discuss in my book **Unraveling Deception**), God will bring forth other encounters for a person to hear the Truth based upon sound, Scriptural teaching. After all, since everything operates within God, He, of course, can bring forth whatever He pleases. That is why the man or woman who prays to be used by God and to meet someone new throughout the week to share the Gospel is most likely going to get that chance. God works through us, His temples, to share and bring forth Truth. The unbeliever that God brings into the life of a praying man or woman could very well be the person who is seeking Truth, but hasn't heard about the one, true Christ.

"Or do you despise the riches of His goodness, forbearance, and longsuffering, not knowing that the goodness of God leads you to repentance?" (Romans 2:4 NKJV). Once the omnibenevolence of God pierces the heart and sinks into the deep waters of our soul, we are brought to a place of longing to turn from that which is ungodly and turn to what is godly. Just as our Father in Heaven is Holy, so we want to be holy. When we see that "God so loved the world that He gave His only begotten Son, that whoever believes in Him should not perish but have everlasting life" (John 3:16 NKJV), how could we sit idly by and not strive to live the lives we were intended to live for God? Love not merely led Christ to the Cross, but it was humility that kept Christ on the Cross. Christ could have at any time said, "these scoffers, idolaters, murderers, sinful, perverse, wicked men and women are not worth it." Christ could have called Himself off that Cross at any point and annihilated man. Instead, it is our omnibenevolent Lord and Savior Who said, ""Father, forgive them, for they do not know what they do"" (Luke 23:34 NKJV). What unlimited goodness found in the roots of humility and love were displayed through those words from Christ. How can we hear those words and not see that God is truly omnibenevolent? His goodness has no bounds or limitations! Great is He that is in us!

God's goodness is not merely seen within the physical realm, it transcends beyond what we see in the physical realm. Many times, we go through life not knowing what God has saved us from. We may become frustrated that our car was not working for the day, but could it be that if we drove on that day we would have gotten into a terrible accident? We become sad when our games get canceled from thunderstorms, but is it God doing so to keep us from injuring ourselves with a tear or break? Maybe a lifelong friend begins to grow distant – could it be that God is allowing this to happen because they would keep us from progressing towards the Lord and deepening our relationship with Him? There are so many variables and so many circumstances that happen along the way of our lives that are confusing and make us upset. Without us knowing, these very instances are part of God painting the perfect picture of our lives and keeping us from harm. God knows when we are to be called Home. Until that time, let us open our eyes to see that God is always working. The way He works may not be ideal according to our standards, but we must know and believe that His omnibenevolence is perfectly orchestrating our lives based upon His omniscience and omnipotence.

We must always remember that "Every good gift and every perfect gift is from above, and comes down from the Father of lights, with Whom there is no variation or shadow of turning" (James 1:17 NKJV). Every good gift we receive comes from the Lord. Our parents may bless us with a gift, but it is actually from God Who operates through our parents to give us that gift. When we are fed for the day and have a roof over our heads, that is God's blessing to us. When we are given friends of Christ-like character and are provided a job that pays for the needs that must be met we can be sure that God's omnibenevolence is at work. Though God puts all of us in different situations, we can trust that the Omnibenevolent God will always be there for the man or woman that diligently seeks His face. Every prayer that is answered and every miracle that is experienced comes from His very hand. As He hears our prayers and sees our needs, He moves His hand in one peaceful stroke. He opens our eyes to see that it is from Him that such goodness comes. Whether a gift or blessing is received eternally or internally, it is all rooted by the One and Only Omnibenevolent God.

Let us therefore shout with praises that the God of all is the God of all good. Goodness does not exist without God. Since everything exists in God, all goodness proceeds from Him. Nothing is outside His reach. Nothing is too hard for Him to perform. If our hearts are willing and our prayers are bold enough to ask for the impossible, then, through the will of God, we can know that He will answer. "With the Lord one day *is* as a thousand years, and a thousand years as one day" (2 Peter 3:8 NKJV). When prayers are answered, they are not always immediately met. God's omnibenevolence operates within His time according to His will. Some of us are not ready to receive the prayer in which we were led by the Holy Spirit to pray. Nonetheless, it does not mean that the answer has not already been given.

"For I know the thoughts that I think toward you, says the LORD, thoughts of peace and not of evil, to give you a future and a hope" (Jeremiah 29:11 NKJV). God is ready and prepared to move upon the hearts that are engaged to fulfill His predestined plan. Our Omnibenevolent God has plans of hope and a future for us. May God grant us the eyes to see His goodness everywhere and in all things. May He reveal to us deeper revelations of His unlimited goodness. May all come to know the Omnibenevolent God Who calls each one of us to Him; Who has a special plan to fulfill through our lives; Who has a new name He will give to us when we enter the gates of Heaven.

O let us "taste and see that the LORD *is* good; Blessed *is* the man *who* trusts in Him!" (Psalm 34:8 NKJV).

* * *

GOD, *we are so grateful for Your omnibenevolence. We thank You that You loved us while we were still sinners. Lord, before we were born, You had predestined plans for us. God, may we continue to seek after Your will. May You draw our hearts closer to You and may You give us minds that receive Your vision. We long to live our lives for You, Father. O God, how Your Omnibenevolence is displayed through the sending of Your Spirit into us wretched sinners who believe in Christ as Lord and Savior. How great and splendid are Your ways to move within our being to sanctify and restore us.*

Lord, we are grateful for Your unlimited goodness that is seen throughout our lives. We thank You for Your saving grace that was presented to us through the atoning sacrifice of Christ. Lord, even when we cannot see Your omnibenevolence at work, we trust You are working all things out for good. Praise be to You, God, for calling every one of us to You. May all see Your unlimited goodness. May all come to know You. In Jesus' name, Amen.

QUOTES FOR MEDITATION

1. "With the goodness of God to desire our highest welfare, the wisdom of God to plan it, and the power of God to achieve it, what do we lack? Surely we are the most favored of all creatures." **A.W. Tozer**

1. "Remember the goodness of God in the frost of adversity." **Charles Spurgeon**

1. "But a faithful believer will in all circumstances meditate on the mercy and fatherly goodness of God." **John Calvin**

1. "Providence so orders the case, that faith and prayer come between our wants and supplies, and the goodness of God may be the more magnified in our eyes thereby." **John Flavel**

1. "There is no creature so small and abject, that it representeth not the goodness of God." **Thomas a Kempis**

OMNISCIENT

ALL-KNOWING

"O Lord, You have searched me and known me. You know my sitting down and my rising up; You understand my thought afar off. You comprehend my path and my lying down, And are acquainted with all my ways. For there is not a word on my tongue, But behold, O Lord, You know it altogether."
— **Psalm 139:1-4 NKJV**

GOD IS ALL-KNOWING. Through His mighty intellect, His wisdom proceeds. In His mind is found a never-ending fountain of knowledge. When His eyes gaze upon us, He knows us more than we will ever know ourselves. Why? Because He created us. Does not the Creator of His creation know everything about what He has created? In the depths of our heart, God is there. He sees that which we long for, that which we desire. God wants to show us what He knows about ourselves. He longs to reveal to us the secret plans and promises He has for each of us. He desires to show us His predestined purpose for our lives. We simply must be open to the Omniscient Mind that longs to share such treasures and jewels.

Not only does God know us better than we know ourselves, He

knows what will happen within our lives before it happens. God, in His omniscience, knows the many possible avenues we could take. He knows the times we will seek Him and choose the right path, as well as the times we will stumble and fall and disregard His teachings and insight. Though God knows what is best, we do not always press into His best. This world in which we live is filled with distractions and temptations at every turn. As our minds engage and interact with God Almighty in an unprecedented way through private prayer, we develop a strong sense of belonging. We begin to understand what life is all about. It is tough, however, to step into the world without being readily equipped with the Word of God. That is why it is so important both to start and end the day with prayer. When we don't spend time with God, we fall prey much more easily to the attacks and temptations of the enemy. Even the mightiest of saints had struggles and fell. Our omniscient God knows when struggles and temptations are to arise, and He *always* provides a way of escape (1 Corinthians 10:13).

"Why doesn't God stop this from happening?", you may ask. If He were to do so at every turn, we would no longer be blessed with the gift of libertarian freewill. We would be pre-programmed robots instructed to do as our diel directs. God, in His omniscience, knows that true love is found in freedom of the will. True love is not forced, for that is rape. Instead, true love has the ability to choose to love. True love is action set into motion through the heart's desire of seeking, serving, obeying, and loving God. True love is a sacrificial life of servanthood that is directed towards good and heartfelt interactions with others, despite opposition, neglect, or hatred from another. God's omniscient mind reveals to us that the one thing that we can always have and that no one can take away from us, aside from the Holy Spirit, is love. God revealed this very love through His Son, the Lord Jesus Christ, as He went to the Cross willfully and with all love. He was not focused on the torment to come or the ridicule and mockery that had happened. Instead, Christ saw past all those things. His love performed an action of servanthood, which led to Him sacrificing His life. God's omniscience knew that many would still reject the Truth, but thanks be to God that He thought it was worth saving you and I, sinners saved by grace through faith (Ephesians 2:8-9).

It is a miraculous truth that God's omniscience is derived not just from His Being but is seen through His aseity and being atemporal. God's omniscience is not just Who He is, but His omniscience is sling-shot into the future of eternity, forever looking back towards the present. His omniscience knows everything that is to come because He Himself has already been and is already there. "Before a word is on my tongue, behold, O LORD, You know it altogether" (Psalm 139:4 ESV). God's eternality allows Him to see forever forward and back-wards. His mind and Being are forever in the past and in the future, simultaneously. Since God has no beginning, He has no end. He is currently in the future, just as He is in the past. God not only is omnipresent within "the present now", but He is also omnipresent within time itself. This Truth brings forth clarity into understanding God's omniscience. God's knowledge springs from already having been, and already being "there". Since everything exists inside God and moves and operates within His eternality, God is all-knowing. There is nothing that God does not know. If God did not know some-thing, then He would not be God. There is only one Alpha and Omega. There is only one First and Last. There is only one Beginning and End, and that is the Lord Jesus Christ.

God's omniscience not only knows all, but cares about all. "He counts the number of the stars; He calls them all by name. Great *is* our Lord, and mighty in power; His understanding *is* infinite" (Psalm 147:4-5 NKJV). Nothing is out of reach, nor too much for God. His comprehension is endless. Why does God include the genealogy within the Scriptures? Not only to bring validation that the Scriptures are true, but to show that His omniscient mind forgets no one. He is the God that knows even the numbers of hairs on our head (Luke 12:7 & Matthew 10:30). What other being knows that number? It is a simple concept to comprehend, yet, not even you or I know the number of hairs on our head.

The Lord truly knows everything about everything because His heart of compassion and love for that which He has created brings forth His omniscience. God is all His attributes all at once. The correlation between love and omniscience brings forth the love and care for even the most minute details that mankind is accustomed to overlooking and disregarding. God overlooks nothing. He knows all not simply because He created all, but because He loves all. Everything is precious to Him because it is derived from His spoken Word and creativity. God needs not one thing, for in His solitariness and aseity His needs are met within Himself and by Himself alone. However, this does not mean that He neglects that which has come from Him.

"Have you not known? Have you not heard? The everlasting God, the LORD, The Creator of the ends of the earth, Neither faints nor is weary. His understanding is unsearchable" (Isaiah 40:28 NKJV). God's omniscience is never exhausted, but forever in a continual state of "knowing". The Lord's stamina and energy from knowing everything forever rests in a constant state of "full". Nothing is extracted, nor does anything additional enter God. He never grows tired, for His entire Being is supplied and stationary within Himself. What comes out of God that is seen by us has already been for Him (Ecclesiastes 3:15). Nothing new can enter Him, when viewed from His eternality. Nothing can be learned by God, for God is Knowledge and Wisdom Himself. He cannot teach *Himself* something new, though He can show *us* something new. God knows when the appropriate time is to reveal a deeper revelation of Himself to us, even though the revelation has always been. Our finite minds simply receive from the omniscient God that which is already of God and known by God.

Glory be to God that He Himself is Knowledge and Wisdom. God knows all because all things reside within Him. God sees all because He created all. God knows the future because the future resides within His eternality. God's mind cannot be contained, and His Being cannot be understood. To have this precious truth sink into the inner chambers of the heart excites the imagination. It provides us with confidence in the One Who spoke a Word and life came into existence. Glory be to God.

* * *

HEAVENLY FATHER, how great it is to worship such a mighty God. Lord, Your omniscience has no limits. How splendid it is to walk through this life knowing that You know all. What a miraculous and marvelous truth it is for our finite minds to comprehend! Lord, we ask that You share that wisdom and knowledge with Your children. Lord, we want the Holy Spirit to speak to the depths of our hearts. May the wisdom that comes from Him forever grow into deeper revelations of Who You are. Lord, You are worthy of worship. We are grateful that we worship the One True God, the Alpha and Omega. Glory be to You, forevermore, O God of Heaven and earth. In Jesus' name, Amen.

QUOTES FOR MEDITATION

1. "God, possessing supreme and infinite wisdom, acts in the most perfect manner, not only metaphysically, but also morally speaking, and ... with respect to ourselves, we can say that the more enlightened and informed we are about God's works, the more we will be disposed to find them excellent and in complete conformity with what we might have desired." **Gottfried Leibniz**

2. "Let me remind you that this is God's universe, and He is doing things His way. You may think you have a better way, but you don't have a universe to rule." **J. Vernon McGee**

3. "Divinity is in its omniscience and omnipotence like a wheel, a circle, a whole, that can neither be understood, nor divided, nor begun nor ended." **Hildegard of Bingen**

4. "God knows instantly and effortlessly all matter and all matters, all mind and every mind, all spirit and all spirits, all being and every being, all creaturehood and all creatures, every plurality and all pluralities, all law and every law, all relations, all causes, all thoughts, all mysteries, all enigmas, all feeling, all desires, every unuttered secret, all thrones and dominions, all personalities, all things visible and invisible

in heaven and in earth, motion, space, time, life, death, good, evil, heaven, and hell." **A.W. Tozer**

5. "Future contingents cannot be certain to us, because we know them as such. They can be certain only to God whose understanding is in eternity above time. Just as a man going along a road does not see those who come after him; but the man who sees the whole road from a height sees all those who are going along the road at the same time." **Thomas Aquinas**

OMNIPOTENT

✎

ALL-POWERFUL

"Also henceforth I am He; there is none who can deliver from My hand; I work, and who can turn it back?""
— *Isaiah 43:13 ESV*

THERE IS NOT one single entity or creation that can overthrow the Master in Whom we know to be God. His omnipotence is unmatched and has no rival. Though a lion is the king of the jungle, there are still those that roam who are taller, stronger, faster, and of more weight than the lion. God, however, is the King, Ruler, and Ultimate Authority over all of Heaven and all of earth. His mind transcends that which has been created and understood by the finite mind. His Being extends beyond that which we have yet to experience.

Though the lion rules with authority, God rules in all aspects. There is nothing that is wider, longer, taller, wiser, or more powerful than God. Within less than one spoken word, God could annihilate mankind. He could send fire as He did upon Sodom and Gomorrah to cleanse the earth of all wickedness. Yet, He remains faithful and just, not wanting any to perish but all to come to repentance (2 Peter 3:9). This truth is an attribute within an attribute. God's power is not only unmatched with power itself, but His power to love others resembles true power. "To whom much is given, from him much is expected" (Luke 12:48). Since nothing has been given by God that He does not already own, we can always expect Him to do what He wills. He neither answers to us, nor anything else that is known to mankind. God is in a constant, perpetual, immutable cycle of answering to Himself. His perfection radiates throughout His Being. Through His perfection, His power can be seen; not just in what has already been accomplished, but what is metaphysical in nature.

Love and self-control can be found in God's power. The power to not smite man every time they sin is seen through the power of His love for us in forsaking His One and Only Son upon the Cross to die for our sins. True power is not simply the ability to do as one pleases, which, in God's case, is always just and perfect. True power is the ability to love the unlovable. The power to love wicked, carnal men who deserve damnation. This same power comes from God, falls upon the true convert, and flows through the veins of those who seek to love others in the same manifestation. Though only One Being has the power to love perfectly, we can have a touch of that love from the Holy Spirit. We can seek and grow in an intimate relationship with the Holy Spirit. Coming to know the Holy Spirit more gives us the power to love others in the same way that Christ loves us.

God's power is not just unsearchable, it is unfathomable. We cannot comprehend the Supreme Being Who has power in which we know nothing about. His omnipotence is greater than any ruler or kingdom. Within a single breath He could send fire upon all the king-doms of all the ages and turn them to dust. Not even the gates of Hell and Satan can stand against the One Who conquered death and the grave. Why will the Battle of Armageddon be the bloodiest battle? Simply because it will be the spraying of the enemy's blood upon our white garments. Will angels *need* to fight on that day? No. Will angels *need* weapons to use against the enemy? Absolutely not. With a single raise of the hand, Jesus Christ can do all that is necessary to defeat the enemy. With a single word, Christ can capture and chain Lucifer and his legion of demons. The angels will have no fear as they escort the chained enemies before the Great White Throne. For the angels know that it is the Lord that will cast them into the Lake of Fire and Brimstone. When the enemy comes before the Throne, they will be powerless. God, in His omnipotence, will make every knee bow and tongue confess that Jesus Christ is Lord (Philippians 2:10-11). The freewill of every enemy, every man, and every evil spirit will in that moment be stopped. Nothing will argue or fight its way out of kneeling before the Holy, Omnipotent God. Glory be to God for this coming display of His Majesty and Greatness.

"No one is like You, Lord; You are great, and Your name is mighty in power. Who should not fear You, King of the nations? This is Your due. Among all the wise leaders of the nations and in all their kingdoms, there is no one like You" (Jeremiah 10:6-7 NIV). Many in their self-deception, ignorance, and pride will shake before Almighty God. When His everlasting glow of perfect light is seen, every sinful, wicked man's knees will tremble in fear. When the time comes where they see the glory of God, it will be too late for them. Every time a Christian evangelized to them will be but echoes in their conscience throughout all of eternity in the Lake of Fire. How fearful that day will be when God awakens and makes His presence known. God, the Maker of Heaven and earth, will sit upon His Throne judging and separating the righteous found in Christ from the wicked bound to sin and self. How great a display will be for those found in Christ. How fearful for those who disregarded Him.

Not only will the coming day be a display of God's omnipotence, but we can see God's omnipotence now both through the Scriptures and through what can be seen with the human eye. Gaze upon the universe and see the vast complexity and beauty of that which we call "space". What imaginable power it must have been to create such a place. When God created the universe, energy, matter, space, and time were created instantly. God, in His omnipotence, created time itself. What was before that? An eternity past of what we know to be God. He is the only Being to never have been created, but to have always existed. What immense power. To meditate on this very truth alone will bring one to their knees in awe and wonderment.

To have this in mind, "Why is it thought incredible by any of you that God raises the dead?" (Acts 26:8 ESV). Some people are complexed at the thought that Christ could have been raised from the dead. When viewing what God has done, however, this is a simple display of His omnipotence. To have His Son be conceived by the Virgin Mary is also just a touch of His power. These wonderful miracles, when reflected and meditated upon, are not hard to comprehend when we view them as being done by the One Who said:

- ""Let there be light," and there was light." (Genesis 1:3 NIV)
- ""Let there be a vault between the waters to separate water from water."" (Genesis 1:6 NIV)
- ""Let the water under the sky be gathered to one place, and let dry ground appear."" (Genesis 1:9 NIV)
- ""Let there be lights in the vault of the sky to separate the day from the night, and let them serve as signs to mark sacred times, and days and years, and let them be lights in the vault of the sky to give light on the earth."" (Genesis 1:14-15 NIV)
- ""Let the land produce living creatures according to their kinds: the livestock, the creatures that move along the ground, and the wild animals, each according to its kind."" (Genesis 1:24 NIV)
- ""Let Us make mankind in Our image, in Our likeness, so that they may rule over the fish in the sea and the birds in the sky, over the livestock and all the wild animals, and over all the creatures that move along the ground."" (Genesis 1:26 NIV)

Notice God's omnipotence as He created. He did not have a guide or a blueprint. Through His omniscience and omnipotence, He created what He had already planned. At the same moment He created, He named that which was created. He did not reflect on what to call it. Rather, it was given a name at the very moment it was given existence. The Lord did not become exhausted in thinking about what was next. Rather, He already knew what He was going to do because He had already been there and done what was done.

God's omnipotence is correlated to His infinitude. He is forever and has no peak. Therefore, His power has no peak. His power in any given circumstance has already happened for Him, when looking through the lenses of His eternality. Though His power be made known to us within a given time period, His power in the days to come is already known to Him. He already knows what will be said and done by His hand. No one can take away what He will do, for His power rules the future. There is nothing that can get in the way or block God from being the God of the future. Since God rules time and is outside it, He already knows the future, for the future resides in Him.

"All the inhabitants of the earth are accounted as nothing, and He does according to His will among the host of heaven and among the inhabitants of the earth; and none can stay His hand or say to Him, "What have you done?"" (Daniel 4:35 ESV). God's omnipotence gives Him complete authority. He answers to no one. None of us can challenge the Lord's ways, for we cannot see what lies ahead. If we had the power of God, our own wisdom would lead to a perverted power. We would not have the patience to be longsuffering. We ourselves would have ended mankind long ago. We would twist and disrupt the world for the sake of ourselves, rather than to use that power to work out a greater good for all.

If evil were to arise, we would immediately bring "justice" (if we even have the right to believe that we would). God, however, is able to work out all evil, suffering, and pain to a greater good because He knows the end result of everything. He can dictate the appropriate circumstances that must take place and what He will allow to bring out a greater good. With imperfections and not knowing what is to come, we would use the power of God (if we so possessed it) to bring temporal satisfaction. We would have the world revolve around us and meet our conditions. We may believe and think we could help the entire world, but we would not have the omniscient mind to understand that which would work out a greater good. We must be thankful and grateful that all of God's attributes move in unison with each other. One does not overlap, but each compliments the other while remaining complete within itself.

God knows all and rules all. Nothing can escape what He has already predestined to happen. No one can fight Him because no one can hold Him. God is in all and through all (Ephesians 4:6), and therefore has power over everything. Let us "Trust in the LORD forever, for the LORD GOD is an everlasting rock" (Isaiah 26:4 ESV). Let us know that ""with God all things are possible"" (Matthew 19:26 ESV).

* * *

HEAVENLY FATHER, we are thankful that You are the Omnipotent God. We are grateful that no one can stand against You and Your power and Your authority. God, You have the final say in all things. All things come from You. God, You are able to take even the most distraught situations and work them out for good. Lord, Your power is infinite and beyond comprehension. May our souls rest in knowing that You are the unconquerable God. We believe that Your eye sees us each day. We believe that You are calling us to a deeper relationship with You. May Your Omnipotence ignite our souls to be bold and courageous as we walk through this earth as vessels of Light for Your Kingdom. Destroy all fear, anxiety, and timid-ness from our being. Lift us above what we once were. We thank You that Your omnipotence and sovereignty govern and protects our lives. Glory be to You, Father. In Jesus' name, Amen.

QUOTES FOR MEDITATION

1. "This is why the ultimate reason of things must lie in a necessary substance, in which the differentiation of the changes only exists eminently as in their source; and this is what we call God." **Gottfried Leibniz**

2. "Whatever God can do faith can do, and whatever faith can do prayer can do when it is offered in faith. An invitation to prayer is, therefore, an invitation to omnipotence, for prayer engages the Omnipotent God and brings Him into our human affairs. Nothing is impossible to the man who prays in faith, just as nothing is impossible with God. This generation has yet to prove all that prayer can do for believing men and women." **A.W. Tozer**

3. "What do you have to fear? Nothing. Whom do you have to fear? No one. Why? Because whoever has joined forces with God obtains three great privileges: omnipotence without power, intoxication without wine, and life without death." **Francis of Assisi**

4. "The greatest single distinguishing feature of the omnipotence of God is that our imagination gets lost thinking about it." **Blaise Pascal**

5. "The Lord God omnipotent can do anything as easily as anything else. All His acts are done without effort. He expends no energy that must be replenished. His self-sufficiency makes it unnecessary for Him to look outside of Himself for a renewal of strength. All the power required to do all that He wills to do lies in undiminished fullness in His own infinite being." **A.W. Tozer**

SOVEREIGNTY

POSSESSING SUPREME
POWER OR AUTHORITY

"Whatever the Lord pleases, He does, in heaven and on earth, in the seas and all deeps."
— **Psalm 135:6 ESV**

GOD'S SOVEREIGNTY is derived from His omnibenevolence. His rushing current of sovereignty flows through the chambers of His wisdom, love, and goodness. There is not one spec of God's sovereignty that is not intertwined with His other attributes. God's perfection and aseity allow Him to do that which is quintessential. No one may argue against God's sovereignty, for all things come from Him. The presence of His Being allows all to live in Him. Since nothing can escape God's eye or presence, He therefore has full authority and supreme power over all things. He dictates perfectly through His pure knowledge. His holiness flows throughout all that He is. Therefore, anything that contradicts His holiness deserves punishment.

God's love for His creation does not immediately kill man at the very first sign of sin or disobedience. For, as we have mentioned previously, God is longsuffering (2 Peter 3:9). He wants all to come to the knowledge of Him. Therefore, He convicts and chastises men and women based upon their misconduct. God, in His omnipotence, created the appropriate consequences for sin. No one is free from sin. Though some sins provide less consequences, in God's eyes, every sin is a disgust. Sin is a stench in His nostrils and is an abominable evil in His sight. Every time we sin, God acts appropriately through the realm in which He operates. He does not smite us at first sin. Instead, He provides the best form of consequence to work as a means of discipline and drawing us (back) to Him. Through everything God does, we are at the forefront of His mind. His sole purpose of operating through His sovereignty is to show mankind that He is merciful and wants a living relationship with each person He has made in His image. Continually, He warns us to flee from the wrath to come (Luke 3:7 & Matthew 3:7).

"Have I any pleasure in the death of the wicked, declares the Lord GOD, and not rather that he should turn from his way and live?" (Ezekiel 18:23 ESV). God wants all of mankind to turn from their wicked ways and run into His blessed promises. He wants each man and woman's name to be written in the Book of Life. However, He wants them to make the decision of accepting Him, independently. Though He draws us to the decision of making a choice about Christ, He Himself does not make us make our choice. God simply provides the necessary means by which we can come to know Him. Some of us feel the blow of conviction from sin so much so that we reach a point where we know we are depraved and in need of a Savior. Others may be so depressed in life that they hear the call of Him Who died upon the Cross for our sins and enter into a living relationship with the Father. Some who possess an analytical mind may come to the realization that Christianity is a logically coherent religion and does in fact contain much evidence that it is true. Whatever the case may be for each individual person, God moves throughout His Being and works His sovereignty to draw man to Him.

Once God does all He can, eventually, through His foreknowledge, He reaches a point where He knows that man will either come to Him or not come to Him through their libertarian freewill. Those who use their libertarian freewill to reject God will be without excuse come

Judgment Day. "For His invisible attributes, namely, His eternal power and divine nature, have been clearly perceived, ever since the creation of the world, in the things that have been made. So they are without excuse" (Romans 1:20 ESV). God does everything in His power to draw man to Him. He knows that in order to have a genuine love for Him, He must allow man and woman to either reject Him or believe in Him. This libertarian freewill decision is only applicable if God's sovereignty has been applied and given one the ability to do so.

"The earth is the LORD's and the fullness thereof, the world and those who dwell therein, for He has founded it upon the seas and established it upon the rivers" (Psalm 24:1-2 ESV). God has the power to do as He pleases without constraint. There is no higher being that can challenge His ways. There is no being that is wiser than Him Who never had a beginning. Only God is the Timeless Being that is perfect in all His ways. As God spoke things into being, His omnificence was revealed as His omnipotence was guided by His omniscience. As God created, He did not wonder what the laws would be or what fair judgment would look like. By His foreknowledge, He already knew what must be done. He designed everything in such a way where He knew the role He would play within His design. For it is only by Him that perfect peace and harmony can exist. God knew that one day He would have to crucify His Son to provide a way for man to come to know Him. God knew that His independent moral agents, Adam and Eve, would soon fall and that much wickedness and evil would occur in the world (Genesis 3). God knew this but did not have to prepare for it. He already had the perfect plan of what would be done at each given point in time for each person to be *drawn* to Him.

God's sovereignty is what dictates the entirety of this universe. Sovereignty without omniscience would breed irresponsibility; something that we ourselves would fall prey to if given the opportunity. God's attributes, however, are always intertwined. He Himself moves all at once, using the perfection of each attribute in its perfect time. Wrath and love cannot be done without sovereignty. However, wrath and love can be done apart from each other. God's omniscience is the guiding attribute that separates love and wrath from operating towards the same object. Since God has this innate privilege of possessing sovereignty over all, He is able to direct His ways in a manner that does not distort His power, but uses it in a pure and transcending manner. God's Sovereignty is done in such a way where man cannot comprehend its full effects but trusts in God's omnibenevolence and omniscience that all that is done *by* Him is done *for* Him. He does not do what is unjust, for what is wrong and impure contradicts His Holy Being. God's sovereignty is a sensitive nerve towards that which is immoral and wicked. His character does not love that which contradicts His nature. He despises it. Therefore, it is the Infinite One Who possesses unlimited sovereignty that distributes appropriate actions towards specific circumstances.

""I know that You can do all things, and that no purpose of Yours can be thwarted"" (Job 42:2 ESV). As long as mankind has been alive, Satan has done all he can to try and place himself above God and destroy man. Satan's self-deception is derived through his blinding pride. As he views himself mightier than God, he falsely convinces himself that he can defeat God and drift Him from His purposeful plan with mankind. What a tragic story it is when viewing Satan. The greatest angel who became the greatest devil. It was the transition of a hierarchical fall; going from a pure mindset to a distorted one. It was freewill used in a distraught manner. It was through this inner inclination from Satan that he became the fallen angel. Even though God knew the time would come, His heart was grieved when His most blessed angel turned his back on Him!

God's Sovereignty is clearly displayed and easily recognized to all of mankind through the atoning sacrifice of Jesus Christ. When we repent and believe, we all can see that man is no longer bound by sin but bound by the timeless act of Christ's crucifixion. Through the Blood our soul is stored away in God's unreadable Book. There is only One Who may read of that heavenly language where we will be given a new name (Revelation 2:17). There is only One Whose Blood is the ink of the names written in the Book. It is the Lord Jesus Christ Who has provided the means of our name to be both written and protected until the day it is read before all the people of all the ages (Revelation 3:5).

O how great and mighty and powerful is the Lord Jesus Christ! "He is the radiance of the glory of God and the exact imprint of His nature, and He upholds the universe by the word of His power. After making purification for sins, He sat down at the right hand of the Majesty on high, having become as much superior to angels as the name He has inherited is more excellent than theirs" (Hebrews 1:3-4 ESV). By a single word, God upholds the cosmos. Mankind is living due to the laws instituted by God's very wisdom. Salvation for men who deserve damnation was brought forth to all humans who would repent and believe Jesus Christ is Lord and Savior. It is God Who "has spoken to us by His Son, Whom He appointed the heir of all things, through Whom also He created the world" (Hebrews 1:2 ESV). No greater being exists than Jesus Christ Himself. He is Lord of all and is the Possessor of permanent and complete sovereignty. He is the ineradicable God Whose life will forever be ineffaceable.

What glorious wonder and awe will be found for those in Heaven who meditate upon Christ's life throughout eternity. What horror and discouragement will be for those bound to Hell who refused to accept the simplicity of the Cross. May God give us peace and trust as we meditate on His sovereignty. He rules all because He is the Creator of Heaven and earth (Genesis 1:1).

Let us remember that ""with God, all things are possible"" (Matthew 19:26 ESV). Let us remember that greater is He that is in us than he that is in the world (1 John 4:4). May we forever acknowledge to God that "all things come from You, and of Your own have we given You" (1 Chronicles 29:14 ESV). We cannot give that which already belongs to God. All we can do is simply possess it and return it with a pure spirit. It is our willingness to allow the soul to under-stand that all we are and all we have is by God's Sovereignty. He does not bring something into our life, without first allowing it and having a reason behind it. It is through His sovereignty that we can see and comprehend this truth because God possesses supreme power and authority. He not only judges righteously, but He operates throughout our lives holistically. His authority is impeccably used in the now because He has possessed sovereignty since the time of His infinite past.

Glory be to Him Who possesses that which no being can change, take, or challenge.

* * *

HEAVENLY FATHER, we come before You grateful for Your immaculate sovereignty that rules the foundations and dimensions of all we know. There is nothing You do without reason. All power and authority belong to You. Only You, O God, can use Your power perfectly for all eternity. No man can argue or go against that which is already Yours. Great are You, Father. We give You all the glory and praise for Your guidance and appropriate consequences that bring us closer to You. May Your will forever be done. For we know that Your will is guided by Your wisdom and love. Raise up the righteous, through the blood of Christ, God. Draw us to a deeper understanding of the power that saves man from Hell and brings forth the capability of having a living relationship with You. May Your name forever be praised. In Jesus' name, Amen.

QUOTES FOR MEDITATION

1. "By 'God', I understand, a substance which is infinite,
   independent, supremely intelligent, supremely powerful,
   and which created both myself and everything else...that
   exists. All these attributes are such that, the more carefully I
   concentrate on them, the less possible it seems that they
   could have originated from me alone. So, from what has
   been said it must be concluded that God necessarily exists."
   Rene Descartes
2. "When you go through a trial, the sovereignty of God is the
   pillow upon which you lay your head." **Charles Spurgeon**
3. "Although the sovereignty of God is universal and absolute,
   it is not the sovereignty of blind power. It is coupled with
   infinite wisdom, holiness, and love. And this doctrine, when
   properly understood, is a most comforting and reassuring
   one. Who would not prefer to have his affairs in the hands
   of a God of infinite power, wisdom, holiness, and love,
   rather than to have them left to fate, or chance, or
   irrevocable natural law, or to short-sighted and perverted
   self? Those who reject God's sovereignty should consider
   what alternatives they have left." **Loraine Boettner**

4. "A consciousness of our powerlessness should cast us upon Him who has all power. Here then is where a vision and view of God's sovereignty helps, for it reveals His sufficiency and shows us our insufficiency." **Arthur W. Pink**

OMNICOMPETENT

⚜

ABLE TO JUDGE & DEAL WITH ALL MATTERS

"If the Lord search the heart and test the mind, to give every man according to his ways, according to the fruit of his deeds.""
— *Jeremiah 17:10 ESV*

GOD IS the ultimate Judge and Authority. He rules over all because all that is has come from Him.

Since God has created all we know, He therefore is able to judge all we know. Nothing escapes what God can see, for everything that He sees exists within Him. God exerts no stress or wonderment in how to perform His judgment upon a person or upon a nation. God's omnicompetence comes from His love; though, His omnicompetence is also expressed through His justice. Since nothing takes God by surprise, He acts accordingly to that which He has already foreseen.

As man speaks, God listens. As man acts, God sees. As man thinks, God dwells. There is no place in which one can escape the High and Holy One. He dwells within the realm of realms. His understanding flows through all. His dealing with all matters is as easily done as a mathematician solving $1 + 1$. Nothing exerts or stresses God, for how can stress dwell in Him Who is omniscient and omnipotent?

Our understanding of God must be met with the like-mindedness of David and Solomon: ""And you, Solomon my son, know the God of your father and serve Him with a whole heart and with a willing mind, for the Lord searches all hearts and understands every plan and thought. If you seek Him, He will be found by you, but if you forsake Him, He will cast you off forever" (1 Chronicles 28:9 ESV).

God hides from no one, for He can be easily seen in that which He has created (Romans 1:20). God knows and understands the words that come out of our mouths before they are originated into a thought of being spoken.

If God foreknows all, He can judge all. For those who seek after God, He will not hide Himself from them. He will not leave them to go through this life on their own or in their own strength. God is gracious to the spirit that is lowly of heart (Isaiah 57:15). He loves the imperfect, finite creature that is humble enough to admit their depraved state. It is our Heavenly Father Who deals with those who possess this mindset with all grace, mercy, love, and truth.

God directs His omnicompetence perfectly within our lives. As we progress through our Christian walk, we are bound to stumble and fall. This is not an excuse for sinning. Rather, a recognition of our finite being. Our spirit is willing, but our flesh is weak (Matthew 26:41).

When we fall, God helps us up in love. Sometimes, this love must be met with discipline. "For the Lord disciplines the one He loves, and chastises every son whom He receives" (Hebrews 12:6 ESV). At the moment of our conversion, we can expect that conviction will set in. God, in His omnicompetence, will convict us in love and in segments. He does not convict us of all our wrong, all at one time. To do so would give us the feeling of falling so short, that we would ask ourselves what would be the point in seeking to walk the path of Christ? It would implant in us the thought that, "there is no way I can do this. I'm so far from where the Lord is calling me to be." Though we all fall short of what God is calling us to be, there is a process by which God deals with each of us independently.

God's omnicompetence first directs us to getting rid of the essentials. By essentials, I mean those who are sexually immoral, fornicators, idolaters, adulterers, men who practice homosexuality, orgies, thieves, drunkards, revilers, swindlers, murderers, sorcerers, and those who are envious, greedy, jealous; full of enmity and anger (1 Corinthians 6:9-10, Galatians 5:19-21, Ephesians 5:5, Revelation 21:8, Revelation 22:15). God first convicts us of all these things. Then, He gives us the power from the Holy Spirit to cast these far from us. Once these have gone and no longer take root as habitual sins, God moves into the "second layer" of conviction.

Some of these second-layered convictions include:

1. Spending time with family and friends all day long and only spending time with God for a few minutes.
2. Watching movies and reading social media posts for hours and neglecting to read God's Word.
3. Reading and memorizing the Word to appear knowledgeable before men rather than to simply seek and know God.
4. Resisting the Spirit's inner voice of speaking a word of encouragement or helping someone at the expense of completing our normal routine.
5. Finally, the experience of God can even become a form of idolatry. Someone can become so infatuated with the feeling of God's presence, rather than God Himself. We must know that there will be seasons in the Christian life where it feels like God is not there; even though, He is.

God deals with us according to where we are in Him. His balance of conviction and love reveals His willingness to not only meet us where we are, but to chastise and discipline us, in order that we may be brought to where He is calling us.

Christianity is not about perfection, it's about progression. God will always take us where we are, but He will never leave us where we are. God is willing to chastise us in love, in order that we may grow deeper in the richness of His Son, Jesus Christ. God is willing to discipline us in hopes that we accept and thank Him for His discipline, for it is through discipline that we learn what is right and what is wrong. We learn what is fruitful and what is sinful. We learn what is beneficial and what is hindering. We learn what is acceptable and what is distracting. It is those who love discipline who will gain knowledge (Proverbs 12:1). Our Lord's chastisement and discipline are the actions that rest in His Omnicompetence, and they are always done in love.

God's perfect Omnicompetence is not merely done in love, however. It is also done in justice. "For if God did not spare angels when they sinned, but cast them into hell and committed them to chains of gloomy darkness to be kept until the judgment" (2 Peter 2:4 ESV), will He not also deal with all the sinners of all the ages? God's omnicompetence is the locker that holds men's souls. Those who refused to repent and believe in Jesus Christ as Lord and Savior will be judged appropriately. Their portion will be with all the transgressors of all the ages. Worse still, everlasting fire will be their eternal abode. They will be tormented (not tortured) alongside Lucifer and his legion of demons.

God has every right to deal with such men in this exact way. It is not that God never called them to Him. God was willing to forgive. For He longs to forgive all men (2 Peter 3:9). He provided the perfect gift through the atoning sacrifice of His Son. It is man's own pride, neglect, sin, and selfishness that keeps them from entering into the promised salvation that God so longs to give. It is because of the freewill of man that they divert themselves from the blessedness of the Cross to a life that is lost. Their hearts long for instant, temporal satisfaction, but what awaits them is spiritual damnation.

It is sad when the blessed hope of Heaven is forever lost by a failure to acknowledge oneself as a sinner. "But the eyes of the wicked will fail; all way of escape will be lost to them, and their hope is to breathe their last"" (Job 11:20 ESV).

It is a wonderful truth to know that God does not overlook any matter. He is forever present, viewing each person's life. Nothing escapes His knowing. Those who have done wrong and do not have

Christ as their Lord and Savior will face the wrath that is to come (1 Thessalonians 1:10). Murderers who killed, thieves who stole, corrupt politicians, and kidnappers who raped all will have the wrath of God breathe down upon them. There will be no place for them to run once they draw their final breath. Each person's soul will suddenly fall into the hands of either the love of God or the wrath of God.

God's holiness is the bedrock that brings forth one of these two responses. The wrath of God is directed towards those who will be sent to Hell due to refusing to repent and believe in Christ. The love of God is directed towards those who ascend into Heaven through belief in Christ and repentance of their sins.

Those not found in Christ will receive what they deserve. God's omnicompetence will not let them escape the damnation that they built for themselves here in this life. God will have justice done for those who wronged Him and His children. He is the Preeminent Father whom no one can thwart.

It is forever important to know that "a man's ways are before the eyes of the Lord, and He ponders all his paths" (Proverbs 5:21 ESV). God cannot, not see. Nothing escapes His sight. It is this truth that rests in the chamber of God's omnicompetence that should both guide and relieve us. It should guide us towards always doing the right thing. It should alleviate us from the stress and anger of not seeing justice be done for wrong. Though man may escape from his wicked acts for a short time here on earth, his ungodly acts will soon stand before him come Judgment Day.

May God's omnicompetence bring peace to the soul as we know that He will see us through. God ""will never leave you nor forsake you"" (Hebrews 13:5 ESV). He will deal accordingly with all of us at the proper time.

He is the Omnicompetent God. His omniscience and justice are the wings that sore across every soul that is to be judged.

May the response of God's omnicompetence be one of rewards when we see Him on that Final Judgment Day; not because of anything we have done, but because of what Christ did with our genuine, open hearts. For "it is God Who executes judgment, putting down one and lifting up another" (Psalm 75:7 ESV).

* * *

HEAVENLY FATHER, we thank You for Your omnicompetence. We praise You for revealing to us the truth that nothing escapes Your sight. Lord, You see all and You know all. Before something comes into being, You have already been to its place of fruition. We thank You, Lord, that You deal with us in love. Though it be tough love at times, we accept it with full recognition that You are doing so for our good. Lord, may our hearts never be complacent with where we are currently at in You. Continue to do whatever it takes for us to know You as much as we can in this life. Draw us to higher ground, Lord. We look forward to the day where those who have wronged us and refused to repent and believe in You will be judged. Lord, what a frightening day it will be for them. May all come to know You, Lord, before their time is up. You are the Omnicompetent God, and we trust in Your providence to keep us from the enemy. Absorb us into Your Presence, O God. Take that which is not of You and deal with us accordingly. We believe You are always working and always moving. Breath in us newness of life. Guide us according to Your Word. In Jesus' name, Amen.

QUOTES FOR MEDITATION

1. "For things remain possible, even if God does not choose them. Indeed, even if God does not will something to exist, it is possible for it to exist, since, by its nature, it could exist if God were to will it to exist." **Gottfried Leibniz**

2. "It is, therefore, not proper for God thus to pass over sin unpunished." **Anselm of Canterbury**

3. "None are ruined by the justice of God but those that hate to be reformed by the grace of God." **Matthew Henry**

4. "Nothing can tend so much to humble us before the mercy and justice of God as the consideration of His benefits and our own sins. Let us, then, consider what He has done for us, and what we have done against Him; let us call to mind our sins in detail, and His gracious benefits in like manner, remembering that whatever there is of good in us is not ours, but His, and then we need not be afraid of vainglory or of taking complacency in ourselves." **Francis of Assisi**

5. "When we look at the cross we see the justice, love, wisdom, and power of God. It is not easy to decide which is the most luminously revealed, whether the justice of God in judging sin, or the love of God in bearing the judgment in our place,

or the wisdom of God in perfectly combining the two, or the power of God in saving those who believe. For the cross is equally an act, and therefore a demonstration, of God's justice, love, wisdom, and power. The cross assures us that this God is the reality within, behind and beyond the universe." **John Stott**

OMNIPARIENT

PRODUCE OR BRING FORTH ALL THINGS

"*or by Him all things were created that are in heaven and that are on earth, visible and invisible, whether thrones or dominions or principalities or powers. All things were created through Him and for Him.*"
— *Colossians 1:16 NKJV*

WHATEVER WE SEE or understand comes from God. By God, and God alone, all things have come into being and have been produced. Whether it is the physical realm in which we see, or it is the spiritual realm in which we feel and experience, God made both for His glory. Though the libertarian freewill of man destroyed God's original plan, God has allowed all the wrong and sin in this world to happen, in order that He may bring about a beautiful story for His glory. This is clearly portrayed from Genesis to Revelation - God turning evil and working it out for a greater good.

"By the word of the Lord the heavens were made, And all the host of them by the breath of His mouth" (Psalm 33:6 NKJV). We can distinguish three overarching objects that were made by our Omniparient God: The earth, the heavens, and mankind. Each of these has a collection of magnificent attributes, detail, and design. Though there are a collection of objects that are referred to as the same (within their given category), not one thing is made the same. There are billions of people who walk this earth. However, not one person is designed the same. There are many animals that roam this world, but not one is the same. Yes, there may be plenty of deer and rabbits that prance and hop through the wilderness, but none of them are identical. Whether its genetic makeup, physical looks, or personality, each design that has been made by God has its own uniqueness.

""Can you bind the cluster of the Pleiades, Or loose the belt of Orion? Can you bring out Mazzaroth in its season? Or can you guide the Great Bear with its cubs? Do you know the ordinances of the heavens? Can you set their dominion over the earth?" (Job 38:31-33 NKJV). Our Lord Jesus is the God of detail. He has fine-tuned this universe to operate to the exact decimal. Stars were not randomly scattered throughout the galaxy. Rather, through God's omniscient mind, He placed them in their proper place for His specific purpose. We may see a cluster of scattered galaxies and stars through pictures of space, but God could sit each one of us down and explain why He brought forth each star that He did and why He placed it there.

Each planet was not placed by mere randomness. Instead, each had a specific purpose for where God placed it. "He stretches out the north over empty space; *He* hangs the earth on nothing" (Job 26:7 NKJV). God not only brought forth the planets themselves, He brought forth the place in which they would dwell. Not only did He bring forth the galaxy in which the planets would reside, He developed the appropriate distance each planet needed to be from the sun. For earth, He created the exact distance in order that habitation could occur, and where life would be both permitted and preserved. Great is the mind of God to not merely bring forth all things, but to design each uniquely and intuitively.

Not only did God bring forth the heavens in which we can see with our physical eyes, He also brought forth the patterns and ways in which they would present themselves. God designed each and everything to reveal His power and might. When God placed the stars within the galaxy, He not only placed them where His omniscient mind saw fit; He also gave them a particular job to do. "For thus says the Lord, Who created the heavens, Who is God, Who formed the earth and made it, Who has established it, Who did not create it in vain, Who formed it to be inhabited: "I *am* the Lord, and *there is* no other" (Isaiah 45:18 NKJV). There is no greater being mightier than He Who created both heaven and earth. God provided every physicality and motion to have its own unique, specific purpose.

There is no greater mind than the One Whose mind is not bound by time. For us to even have thoughts, God Himself must rule and reign within the dimension of thought itself. Since He is inescapable and His mind is impenetrable, then all that we perceive is new and innovative is actually God's thoughts being shared with ours and set into motion. That which is brought forth by man is technically brought forth by God, because God has given each person the ability to be creative and intelligent. These two aspects do not come from mere man. For that which is deemed good and original, is technically unoriginal. It is original to man, for man has never thought or seen of that which has yet to come. To God, however, everything is unoriginal. He has been to that place where what is to come will suddenly be brought forth. It is His omniparience that shares with us the thoughts that are good and pure; innovative and creative; righteous and holy. He is the Mind of all minds.

"The Lord by wisdom founded the earth; By understanding He established the heavens;" (Proverbs 3:19 NKJV). As we will see further in this book, wisdom is an attribute of God. Wisdom is not something that was created but is something that has always been. Wisdom resides within the mind of God, and it is through this wisdom that earth was made. As *wisdom* is knowing the perfect will of what must be done within any given circumstance, *understanding* is recognizing and applying the wisdom that is known. God knew how to create the earth before He created it. God knew how to bring forth that which He was going to create before it was created. God, through His omniscience, knew how it would be done and He did so effortlessly. Recognizing this, it is important to understand this truth: *when God creates, He exhausts nothing.*

God does not become tired or weary. He forever is fully satisfied within Himself. His knowledge and wisdom have no limits. Therefore, He is able to do just as He sees Himself doing in the future. He knows how He will respond and act in the future, yet He is still active in the present. When there was no such thing as time and space before the foundations of the Universe, God already saw this exact moment of you reading this book. He knew how you would feel, what time you would be reading it, and your response to it (which is hopefully good thus far)! He already saw this because everything that exists was *already for* Him. It simply was not brought into fruition and seen by us. Since God has always existed, every moment is present to Him. Fast forward one hundred years from now and God is already there. He knows what will happen. He sees that which He has created. Within this exact moment, He is present in the future just as He is present right now. Since God is the Creator of time itself, He has full reign to move as He pleases within the realm of time.

Since time was created, that means God must be greater than time. Time cannot outrun God, for God is both in time and outside time. If all of time as we know it were concealed in a 24-hour clock, God is the one holding the clock. He sees all the dials. He sees when He chose to create time and when time itself will end. He sees all of it as clear as we can see the watch on our wrist. Though, we only see the dials and what time it is on the watch of our wrist, God sees all the situations and responses throughout time. He sees the good and the evil. He sees His creation, as well as the new beginnings and endings of each person. He sees every living thing and each event that is to come, all at once. Nothing is outside His eye, for in His eye are the foundations of all we know and all we see. This, we can refer to, as the realm of time. Time, simply put, is the existence of every physical beginning tracked to its physical ending.

"When I consider Your heavens, the work of Your fingers, The moon and the stars, which You have ordained, What is man that You are mindful of him, And the son of man that You visit him? For You have made him a little lower than the angels, And You have crowned him with glory and honor. You have made him to have dominion over the works of Your hands; You have put all *things* under his feet, All sheep and oxen—Even the beasts of the field, The birds of the air, And the fish of the sea That pass through the paths of the seas." (Psalm 8:3-8 NKJV). Our Omniparient God has designed us as human beings who are created in His image. Though the Triune God collectively does not have an official image, because God is Spirit (John 4:24), He made us with similar, overlaying characteristics of Him. He has made us in such a way where we have dominion over all that He has created on this earth. He has given us purpose and meaning in this life. He has designed us to be responsible moral agents. God, in His omniscience, has given us the characteristics and capacities to rule. This is all done through the image in which we have been made by Him.

What is this image that makes us like Him? Though we are sinners in need of a Savior, our very image is made known by what God has placed in us. No other creature or living thing on earth possesses what we as humans have; that being, Spirit. "Thus says God the Lord, Who created the heavens and stretched them out, Who spread forth the earth and that which comes from it, Who gives breath to the people on it, And spirit to those who walk on it" (Isaiah 42:5 NKJV). We are spiritual beings encapsulated in a physical, human body. We are not our bodies, but we are our spirit. Our eternal abode is meant to be with God, Who is Spirit. God wants our spirit to be morphed into His forever, even though we will still have bodies that are made new once in Heaven. "For our citizenship is in heaven, from which we also eagerly wait for the Savior, the Lord Jesus Christ, who will transform our lowly body that it may be conformed to His glorious body, according to the working by which He is able even to subdue all things to Himself" (Philippians 3:20-21 NKJV). This can only happen when we believe in Jesus Christ as Lord and Savior and repent.

When this decision is made, we begin to understand that we ourselves belong to God. When we accept Christ, it is the Holy Spirit that comes and breathes newness of life into us. He presents to us new truths. These truths have always been, but they have not always been understood or seen. It takes the first step of faith to walk outside the door of human understanding and into the nature of God's wisdom. It is through our spirit being ruled by the Holy Spirit that we can be pulled out of the world and into the spiritual realm of God's presence. It is the Holy Spirit that lets us know that *"there is* one God, the Father, of whom *are* all things, and we for Him; and one Lord Jesus Christ, through whom *are* all things, and through whom we *live."* (1 Corinthians 8:6 NKJV).

The Lord not only brought forth our very spirit and placed it within our temporal bodies, He specifically made our complex bodies as a vessel to hold our souls for the finite time we reside on earth. "For You formed my inward parts; You covered me in my mother's womb" (Psalm 139:13 NKJV). The Lord Himself designed the complex and perfect construction of mankind. This complexity can be found in the genetic information called DNA. The vast complexity of one single DNA strand still leaves man in awe and wonder. No one has come to fully understand just exactly what DNA is. Yes, we have a solid basis of understanding what it's generality is, but we do not fully comprehend it in its entirety. Knowing that man cannot fully fathom the smallest of things and understand its complexity should make our hearts shout to the Lord in praise and worship! "O Lord, how manifold are Your works! In wisdom You have made them all. The earth is full of Your possessions—This great and wide sea, In which *are* innumerable teeming things, Living things both small and great" (Psalm 104:24-25 NKJV). How marvelous are the works of the Lord to reveal His glory in all things; even the smallest of compounds, such as DNA!

God not only designed each human being, He also creates and brings about the time frame in which each of us are to live (Acts 17:24-29). None of us is promised the next day. Yet, God is gracious. He is the One Who gives breath to our lungs and beats to our heart. He allows us to see, taste, touch, smell, and live. When we are born-again believers, it is the life of God that dwells within the soul of man. Just as Elijah was carried away into the clouds by a chariot to meet God (2 Kings 2), so it is the Holy Spirit that chariots us home when we draw our last breath.

"The Spirit of God has made me, And the breath of the Almighty gives me life" (Job 33:4 NKJV). It is a miraculous work of the Lord to develop the detailed design of breathing. It is the very nature of inhaling and exhaling through our lungs that allows us to remain in a state of consciousness and awareness. God's omniscient mind not only designed the complexity of man but designed him perfectly. God knew the placements of where each organ, muscle, and bone should go without any guide or instruction. He knew simply because He is all knowing. God's omniparience is expressed through His omniscience. Each work that He does is simultaneous with His creativity and knowledge.

Not only does God produce all things within the physical realm, He also produces all that is within the abstract realm: "For behold, He Who forms mountains, And creates the wind, Who declares to man what his thought *is*, And makes the morning darkness, Who treads the high places of the earth—The Lord God of hosts *is* His name" (Amos 4:13 NKJV). The Lord God not only has brought forth that which is physical, but also that which is nonphysical. We may believe that thoughts are our own, but they are simply an extension from His omniscient mind. Evil is the privation of what is good. Sin is rebellion towards God and an attempt to be as He is. When thoughts are sinful and evil, these do not come from the mind of God. Rather, they come from that which is opposite of Him. God is not able to meditate and think on sinful thoughts, for they are an abomination to Him. Sinful thoughts, however, exist due to the fall of Adam. For man to have the libertarian freewill to decide what is right, there must be the possibility of doing that which is wrong.

In regard to a born-again believer's thoughts, we are constantly waging war within our mind. This war is between that which is good and that which is evil. As the Holy Spirit lives in the true born-again believer, their thoughts become purified, altered, and directed by Him. This occurs based upon the authentic seeking of the Father's will by each converted Christian. The Holy Spirit then moves about freely in the abstract realm. That which is good, righteous, and holy is derived from the very mind of God. For that which is holy comes from Him Who is Holy. We cannot think *outside* of God. Although, we can think *apart* from Him. Our thoughts are forever viewed and seen by God. However, that does not mean they originated by God. When we allow thoughts of temptation, evil, and sin to linger and take root within our mind, we are fully responsible. That is why it is important to always seek the will of the Father. For in Him can be found that which is peaceful and perfect.

God's presence and power flows throughout all His creation. Our mind can only operate when we have a fully functioning brain in our skull. For God, however, He is not bound by His physical creation because He is Spirit (John 4:24). His very mind is everywhere that He is. God exists within our thoughts because our very thought life resides within Him. Numbers are abstract. They are derived from the mind of God and have been used as the measurement for virtually all things. Though numbers are not physical, they do help decipher and understand that which is in the physical realm. Numbers, therefore, were brought forth by God in order that we may both better understand and operate within the world around us.

O how great and mighty is He, Who brings forth all things from now and into eternity! "He has made the earth by His power, He has established the world by His wisdom, And has stretched out the heavens at His discretion. When He utters His voice, *There is* a multitude of waters in the heavens: "And He causes the vapors to ascend from the ends of the earth. He makes lightning for the rain, He brings the wind out of His treasuries" (Psalm 135:7). The omniparient God is the reason for why we exist. He gives meaning and purpose to everything that is brought forth. He creates all things effortlessly. He provides what is needed for each given thing that is made. He designs and gives the laws by which each thing must operate. He does this perfectly and intuitively. He needs no guidance, for He Himself is wisdom: "The LORD possessed (Wisdom) at the beginning of His way, Before His works of old" (Proverbs 8:22 NKJV).

To know that God has brought forth all things should flood our soul with a peace that transcends all understanding. We should allow this Truth to rush into our minds and be planted as a firm foundation.

If God has brought it forth, then He knows exactly how it will oper-ate, move, and have its being. If everything was brought forth by God, then surely He sees all that happens. Let our hearts rejoice in the blessed truth that God is omniparient. ""You are worthy, O Lord, To receive glory and honor and power; For You created all things, And by Your will they exist and were created"" (Revelation 4:11 NKJV).

* * *

HEAVENLY FATHER, *great are You and worthy of praise. Lord, we are in awe of Your power. Lord, You are the One and only God. You are the God of Truth that brings forth all things. Nothing exists outside of Your doing. Nothing exists outside of Your presence. Lord, may we give You the honor, praise, and glory that You desire. Without You, we cannot walk one step. It is You alone Who brings life to our souls. It is You alone Who gives meaning and purpose to our lives. Lord, You are marvelous and Your glory is incom-prehensible! On that Blessed Final Day, we will see that this life was just a touch of Your omnificent mind and omniparient power! Great will be that day when we are raised out of sin and brought forth fully into Your presence. May our souls forever rejoice and continue to long for that place which we will call Home. Thank You, Father, for giving us meaning, hope, and a future. In Jesus' name, Amen.*

QUOTES FOR MEDITATION

1. "Thus God alone is the primary Unity, or original simple substance, from which all monads, created and derived, are produced." **Gottfried Leibniz**
2. "Every substance is as a world apart, independent of everything else except God." **Gottfried Leibniz**
3. "There is no inconsistency in God's commanding us not to take upon ourselves what belongs to Him alone. For to execute vengeance belongs to none but Him Who is Lord of all; for when the powers of the world rightly accomplish this end, God Himself does it Who appointed them for the purpose." **Anselm of Canterbury**
4. "Whatever is in motion must be put in motion by another. If that by which it is put in motion be itself put in motion, then this also must be put in motion by another, and that by another again. But this cannot go on to infinity, because then there would be no first mover, and, consequently, no other mover; seeing that subsequent movers move only inasmuch as they are put in motion by the first mover; as the staff moves only because it is put in motion by the hand. Therefore it is necessary to arrive at a first mover, put in

motion by no other; and this everyone understands to be God." **Thomas Aquinas**

5. "I have concluded the evident existence of God, and that my existence depends entirely on God in all the moments of my life, that I do not think that the human spirit may know anything with greater evidence and certitude." **Rene Descartes**

OMNIFICENT

UNLIMITED IN CREATIVE POWER

"*D*o you know how God lays His command upon them and causes the lightning of His cloud to shine? Do you know the balancings of the clouds, the wondrous works of Him Who is perfect in knowledge,*"
— *Job 37:15-16 ESV*

NOT ONLY IS God the Creator of all things, He is also the Creator of creativity itself. All that we see resides in Him because it was made by Him. The realm of creativity itself exists within God. He has made all things without prior instruction. He, therefore, is creative in all that He creates. "It is He Who made the earth by His power, Who established the world by His wisdom, and by His understanding stretched out the heavens" (Jeremiah 10:12 ESV).

God's omnificence can be seen throughout the way in which He creates. God needs to simply think of what He wants to create and it is there. With a single word God perfectly creates that which He knows He wants to create. As it is projected into the physical, spiritual, or abstract realm, it is made specifically as God saw it. His foreknowledge sees that which He will create and how it should be created. To Him, everything is seen from the infinite past to the infinite future, at the same time. He knows what He wants to create at any time and at a specific time. To Him, all things exist simultaneously because He is infinitely timeless. Therefore, nothing can surprise God because He Himself has already seen what He will do. He has already been and exists in that very place where an object will be created.

Mighty is God and flawless is He with His creativity! Everything He constructs and designs is made instinctively and specifically for the glorification of God Himself. Though God has complete glory within Himself alone, it is to our benefit that we can bring Him glory through allowing the Holy Spirit to fill us and move in us.

God's omnificence is best seen not in simply what He creates, but in its very purpose. Clouds that move across the sky reveal His glory. It is God's omniscient mind that constructed the laws of clouds where they would store water and produce rain to satisfy thirst and water crops. This is a beautiful example of God's omnificence. He not only is able to make that which is to be made from nothing, He is the Developer of the laws and how they will operate within the realm that He has placed that very thing. In God's perfect omnificence, He brings forth the laws and commands the balance, motion, direction, being, and purpose of all things. Miraculously, they coexist and move throughout our realm in flawless manner.

Let us venture into the spiritual realm of God's creation, as revealed to us in Revelation 4:2-8 (ESV):

"At once I was in the Spirit, and behold, a throne stood in heaven, with one seated on the throne. And He who sat there had the appearance of jasper and carnelian, and around the throne was a rainbow that had the appearance of an emerald. Around the throne were twenty-four thrones, and seated on the thrones were twenty-four elders, clothed in white garments, with golden crowns on their heads. From the throne came flashes of lightning, and rumblings and peals of thunder, and before the throne were burning seven torches of fire, which are the seven spirits of God, and before the throne there was as it were a sea of glass, like crystal. And around the throne, on each side of the throne, are four living creatures, full of eyes in front and behind: the first living creature like a lion, the second living creature like an ox, the third living creature with the face of a man, and the fourth living creature like an eagle in flight. And the four living creatures, each of them with six wings, are full of eyes all around and within, and day and night they never cease to say, "Holy, holy, holy, is the Lord God Almighty, Who was and is and is to come!'"

How majestic and beautiful it will be to see these four living creatures; but how much greater the splendor and grandeur of hearing them sing, "Holy, holy, holy, is the Lord God Almighty." God specifically designed these mighty beings to bring Him glory. That is their specific duty so long as God is God. Likewise, when we are brought forth into God's presence, through the blood of Christ, our sole duty in Heaven will be to exist with Christ in praise and worship and be joint heirs; forever growing in the knowledge of God and stewarding the new Heaven and new earth.

"So God created man in His own image, in the image of God He created him; male and female He created them" (Genesis 1:27 ESV). God's creativity of making man in His image portrays the complexity and creativity of His design. Though God is beyond what we can conjure up in our head; though we will never fully see Him – for to fully see Him would mean that we ourselves are outside of Him – He has creatively constructed all of us to be made in His image and to *truly* know and grow in Him.

What great power it takes to create something out of nothing. With one Word, God made all organs, muscles, bone, skin, and physical exteriors to work in unison. He did this all while attaching unique, individual characteristics and traits that differ amongst each person He creates. Not only can this be seen physically, but this can also be seen through each person's personality.

Personality is a wonderful representation of God's omnificence. Each person is uniquely brought into this world with a soul and mind that thinks differently from each other. Reactions to certain events and perceptions of the world are varied. Just as a band of tubas would become dull over time, so mankind would be if everyone possessed the same personality. God, in His omniscience and omnificence, knew that variety would bring forth continual advancement through creative conversations and different minds coming together. Just as a band filled with all instruments can perform a masterpiece, so God has performed a masterpiece through the intelligent design of both man's physicality, as well as his personality. However, it does not end here for man.

God's ability to create the vast complexity of man through his physical attributes and complex personality is a marvelous sign of His omnificence. There are many more layers of God's creation, however, that point to His power. To take it a step further, God's ability to make man a living being that can think independently and freely, shows God's willingness to offer us the chance of coming to Him on our own. God does not force us to come to Him. It is evident that to fully dwell in His shadow is to bring forth protection and purpose within our lives. God has given us the ability to think for ourselves, even when He is calling and drawing us to Him within the exterior realm. This realm is operated through God's immanence and omnipresence. When we look around at the profound complexity of creation, we cannot help but to believe that there is a Being of Higher Order that created what we can see. The fine-tuning of life's existence shouts at the soul of every man that they were designed for a specific purpose. God's creativity of revealing Himself to us can be seen through His creation. Yet, designing man in such a way that they can make their own decisions shows His omnibenevolence, wisdom, and love towards man. God knows that for His creation to possess a perfect love for Him, they must be free to think on their own.

It is a blessed truth indeed that God not only created man – his physical being, personality, ability to think, and independent freedom – but He placed him at the perfect time within the world. God did this so that man could make the most impact for God's Kingdom (if he so freely chooses to become a believer). "For we are His workman-ship, created in Christ Jesus for good works, which God prepared beforehand, that we should walk in them" (Ephesians 2:10 ESV). God has paved a way and designed a predestined plan for every single person He has created. When we are genuinely converted and made new, what we say, do, think, and desire are intertwined with God. This simultaneous awareness that is derived from the inner-being of a converted Christian is both whispered and brought about by the Holy Spirit. This happens when the Christian respects, acknowledges, and seeks the will of God.

Our free-will decision to neglect the voice of the Holy Spirit abolishes God's predestined plan of eternal rewards in Heaven. When we choose our ways over God's predestined plans, we rob ourselves of God's rewards. God's omnificence uniquely equips each of us with the proper opportunities and abilities to do that which He wants to do through us in our lives. He gives us unique gifts, talents, and traits to help build His Kingdom. However, that which has been *given* by Him can only be *rewarded* by Him if it is *done* by Him.

God's omnificence of wanting to reveal His glory in His creation is found through His willingness to enact His perfect plan through us. That which hinders His perfect plan in our lives is sin and self. We must be willing to die in order that we may live. God's omnificence is found through this paradox, and it is only Him Who can bring forth and establish a perfect path amid a chaotic world. Only God can do what He has already planned to do. We simply must submit and die to self, in order that we may take up our cross and follow Him into His purposeful plan.

"By faith we understand that the universe was created by the word of God, so that what is seen was not made out of things that are visible" (Hebrews 11:3 ESV). Our Omnificent God not only creates something from nothing, He Himself creates that which is visible from His invisibleness. Before the beginning of the universe, God was. He was not *something* altogether, for that would mean He is an object. Though God is Spirit (John 4:24), spirit is invisible. We cannot collectively know what God is. God portrays His power and certain attributes through what He creates, but God's very Form is invisible. His Formlessness is distinct and apart from that which we can fully understand, comprehend, and see. The visibility of today could not be made known without the invisibility of God Himself. He not only makes something out of nothing, He reveals part of His invisibility and power through that which He creates.

"Therefore, if anyone is in Christ, he is a new creation. The old has passed away; behold, the new has come" (2 Corinthians 5:17 ESV). Each of us is blessed with the gift of a soul and a spirit. As these inter-twine and belong to the spiritual realm, we are able to become a new creature altogether when Christ's Cross is stamped upon our soul. We are brought into the realm of invisibility with God, without fully comprehending or understanding the magnitude of God. God is the only One Who can illuminate Himself and reveal the spiritual realm because He is the spiritual realm Itself. When we are made new and pass from this life, the Holy Spirit will ascend our soul into Heaven to live with the Father. As Heaven is simply the presence of Jesus, Christ's very presence is the invisibility of God coming into sight. It is His blessed touch of grandeur that ignites the soul to be inflamed and dwell within the presence of Him Who cannot be fully seen.

Though each of us will see the Person of Christ; though Christ is God Himself, God is not just Christ. The Trinity, which is the Father, the Son and the Holy Ghost, collectively, is God. It is a blessed Truth to know that when we see the face of Christ, we will be looking into the understandable face of God Himself. God, however, is beyond that which is seen when we see Christ. Not only does the story of Christ coming to pay for the sins of man reveal God's omnificence, it is also found in the very Nature and Person of Christ. When the Logos became Christ, He brought Himself down to our level to pay for our sins, to save us from Hell, and to bring us into fellowship with God the Father. Though Christ was *truly* God and *truly* man on this earth, He was not *fully* God and *fully* man. This recognition allows the believer to know that when we see the face of Christ, we will see the *true* face of God, without seeing the *full* face of God. We will see God in a manner we can understand, but that is merely portrayed in a representation that we can comprehend. God not only is Christ; He is also the Father and the Holy Ghost.

How great is our Omnificent God! How ineffable are His ways. He transcends understanding itself! His power flows from, in, and through Himself to create that which no other mind could imagine. How exciting the blessed Truth is that there is a new heaven and a new earth that is to come (Revelation 21:1). This life is just the beginning of understanding God's omnificence. All throughout eternity we will learn and grow in God. All throughout time He will take His unlimited, infinite supply of omnificence and produce that which has never been seen, heard, or imagined. We will be able to partake in the blessedness of newly created designs. God may even bless each of us with the ability to receive an extra dose of His omnificence to create that which has never been created. The artists will paint skies never before seen. The architects will build around that which has already been created and established by God. The Lord may grant wisdom and knowledge to the teachers and preachers of our day to speak of attributes that have not yet been found and known by man.

The infinite blessedness of God's presence will be enough. Imagine, Heaven will be filled with more joy and understanding then we can possibly comprehend. For in Heaven, we will see His infinite, omnificent mind continually work out never-ending new experiences, knowledge, tastes, sights, smells, and realities. As we prepare for our departure, let us remember that "Every good gift and every perfect gift is from above, coming down from the Father of lights, with Whom there is no variation or shadow due to change. Of His own will He brought us forth by the word of truth, that we should be a kind of firstfruits of His creatures" (James 1:17-18 ESV).

* * *

HEAVENLY FATHER, *great are You in all Your ways. Lord, You alone are the perfect Creator. You alone can create that which has never been known to man or seen by man. Your ways are not our ways, Father. Our hearts melt at the thought of eternity with Christ. We know not the day or hour You are to come, but we look forward to the beginning of the never-ending. To be with You is to live forever. We worship and praise You for Who You are and what*

You have done to save man from sin. We thank You that through Christ's blood, we can deepen our revelations of You. O Omnificent God, bless our hearts with the child-like excitement and curiosity of the hereafter. May that motivate us to allow You to create that which You want in us, through Your Holy Spirit. We bless You, Father. We give You all the glory. In Jesus' name, Amen.

QUOTES FOR MEDITATION

1. "Who gave you the ability to contemplate the beauty of the skies, the course of the sun, the round moon, the millions of stars, the harmony and rhythm that issue from the world as from a lyre, the return of the seasons, the alternation of the months, the demarcation of day and night, the fruits of the earth, the vastness of the air, the ceaseless motion of the waves, the sound of the wind?" **Gregory of Nazianzus**
2. "God thought and things came to be, in-formed: the Divine thought is the complicated womb of all that is. For it's not likely that, like some painter, He conjured up an image from a similar image, having seen beforehand things which His own one mind did not write." **Gregory of Nazianzus**
3. "God the Father, the supreme Architect, had already built this cosmic home we behold, the most sacred temple of His godhead, by the laws of His mysterious wisdom." **Giovanni Pico della Mirandola**
4. "It is God Who is the ultimate reason of things, and the Knowledge of God is no less the beginning of science than His essence and will are the beginning of things." **Gottfried Leibniz**

5. "In whatever manner God created the world, it would always have been regular and in a certain general order. God, however, has chosen the most perfect, that is to say, the one which is at the same time the simplest in hypothesis and the richest in phenomena." **Gottfried Leibniz**

IMPASSABLE

INCAPABLE OF BEING
PASSED OR SURMOUNTED

"Can anyone hide himself in secret places, So I shall not see him?"
says the Lord; "Do I not fill heaven and earth?" says the Lord."
— *Jeremiah 23:24 NKJV*

NOTHING ESCAPES the sight of God because He is in all and through all (Ephesians 4:6).

God Himself consists of the very words "outside", "extend", and "beyond". These words are not apart from Him. Rather, they are derived from Him. These words have no meaning when compared to God Almighty. It is God Who has given these words their meaning.

Anything and everything that is created by God can be passed. Based upon the Second Law of Thermodynamics and the Big Bang, we know that even the universe is in a state of continual expansion. This means that the universe continues to adapt and grow into the realm which man cannot comprehend or understand. As born-again believers, we know this realm to be God.

As the universe grows, it simply is extending into God's Being. It is reaching the point where only God dwells. Once that growth is met, the process continues. Our universe continues to grow into the unknown dimension in which our everlasting God resides.

Everything dwells within God's Being. There is nothing that exists outside of Him. God is the only Being Who possesses the true and full quality of impassability. Nothing extends beyond God, for all realms, dimensions, abstractions, thoughts, physical creations, and spiritual domains are within Him.

God cannot be passed, for He is the Author of travel. Since God is simultaneously in the earth as He is in the heavens, we can trust that nothing surpasses Him. He is everywhere, without moving. He is all that is while remaining externally independent from all that is. Nothing can pass Thee Impassable God. Nothing can hide from the One Who sees all. There is not one thing that can exist, think, or move outside our Impassable God.

Let us imagine for a moment that we are on a ship. All we can see is the sky and water around us. Let this be the illustration of that which is God. We can see the sky and water, but the length to which that extends is infinite. Not only is it infinite, but it possesses that which is invisible. The spaces that exist between the air and that which we see in this analogy are God. That which our eye can see is the space of air, sky, and water around us.

In this example, everything that is seen with the human eye is God, but it is not God entirely. God's impassability extends beyond what the human eye can see. What we see is God, but He goes beyond that which we cannot see. Our minds cannot conceive of different layers of time, space, matter, energy, or light. Our minds are unable to comprehend such realities because we are finite.

There is always another person who is smarter than us. There is always another person who can do more than us. Our finite beings can always be passed by other finite beings. It is not because we are of lesser value. It is simply because we cannot master everything, nor can we truly master anything.

In the eyes of the world, we may become a master at certain hobbies, sports, and professions. Though we may "master" that very thing, there is someone who has been, is, or will be a greater master of that very thing in which we thrive. So long as our souls are attached to these temporal bodies here on earth, we will always be able to be passed. Why? Because our existence in this life is limited.

God, however, cannot be passed. He cannot be overcome in intelligence, power, or being. He is the Infinite Maximum of all that is. He cannot decrease or increase. He is immutable in the mission of His ways, His attributes, and in His Nature. God cannot be passed because God cannot change. He does not alter in Who He is. God is the greatest conceivable Being that has existed for all eternity. Since He possesses that which is infinite and ineffable, then He most certainly is impassable.

""But will God indeed dwell on the earth? Behold, heaven and the heaven of heavens cannot contain You. How much less this temple which I have built!"" (1 Kings 8:27 NKJV). Heaven and the heaven of heavens cannot contain God. This is a statement of vast perplexity as it pertains to the unknown realm in which God resides.

No being created by God has ever existed within this realm. To reach the height of the dwelling place of God's full holiness would immediately evaporate us. We could not come near to the full holiness of that Light nor see It without becoming nothing.

God's holiness in the heaven of heavens is a place that none will ever come to fully understand. It is a place that belongs wholly to God. It is a place where all things come, for it is the place where God speaks something out of nothing. God cannot share this "place" nor allow anyone to come fully into it. It is only He Who is Ineffable that can reside within this ineffable realm of the heavenlies. Only God may dwell, move, and see that realm, for that realm is Him. It is a "place" of marvelous light. Not even the dwelling place of our home in Heaven will give full sight to this Light of lights that comes from the Lord of lords.

God's dwelling of this eternal, infinite, ineffable light reveals that no man or cherubim will ever be able to come into this "place". Since God rules this highest heavenly dimension, it follows that He cannot be passed elsewhere. It is in this blessed "place" where He has brought forth all things. For only He can dwell in a "place" where only He resides and speaks something into existence from nothing.

Let us imagine for a moment that we would try and attempt to pass God. If we were foolish enough to think we could reach that place where "God is not", then our great attempt would have to begin with an incomprehensible distance of travel.

Let us say that we were to travel for ten billion years at light speed in one direction. Our journey is a blast past all that is known to man. After these billions of years are up, we finally reach that place where we would arrive. When viewing God's impassability in comparison to our journey's destination, it will be as if we have taken just one step to start our journey of walking across the entire universe. As the universe continues to expand, it is an impossibility for us to ever catch up to it. Likewise, to try and go in one direction for any length of time, at any rate of speed, is but a step in the universe when trying to reach that place where "God is not".

O how great is our Preeminent Father! We will never *fully* know the God of gods and Lord of lords. He is the Holy One Whose light shines towards all and exists through all, for it comes from Him Who is all. This light is brighter than life itself. Its power would destroy all who would dare enter into Its presence. It is only God Who can dwell in that light, for He is that Light.

Let us forever praise the One Who sent His Son to die upon that Cross, in order that we may begin to learn of our Ineffable God. Let us forever ask God to deepen our understanding of Him. May we forever seek for greater revelations of Him Who forsook His Son, in order that we might have an eternal relationship with Him, our Heavenly Father.

Let us bless the God of impassability, for it is God "Who alone has immortality, Who dwells in unapproachable light, Whom no one has ever seen or can see. To Him be honor and eternal dominion. Amen" (1 Timothy 6:16 ESV).

* * *

HEAVENLY FATHER, You are the God Who cannot be surpassed. You rule and reign in all dimensions and in all realms. O the knowledge that is to be gathered in Heaven of Who You are! We are grateful, Father, for the continued blessings that will be received in Heaven. To always be growing in knowledge and wisdom of Who You are will be our greatest pleasure. How superior You are to all that is, Father. Nothing escapes Your sight or knowing. Nothing can transcend You. You are the Eternal One Who has no limits. You are the Infinite One Who has no bounds. We thank You, God, for calling us into Your presence. We thank You for revealing Truth to our hearts. Give us the seed of continual curiosity of Your Being, Lord God. May we not grow cold and drift from You. Calm our hearts and give rest to our souls as we melt into Your loving arms. We adore You, O Impassable God. In Jesus' name, Amen.

QUOTES FOR MEDITATION

1. "[God] is perfect not only insofar as He is absolute perfection, defining perfection in Himself and from His singular existence and total perfection, but also because He is far beyond being so. He sets a boundary to the boundless and in His total unity He rises above all limitations. He is neither contained nor comprehended by anything. He reaches out to everything and beyond everything and does so with unfailing generosity and unstinted activity." **Pope Dionysius**

2. "God in His essence is unitary and utterly simple, yet ineffably contains multiplicity within Himself: primarily, the triunity of Persons, but also the plenitude of divine attributes, powers, and energies." **Gregory Palamas**

3. "Types and symbols are temporal images pointing to timeless realities which far transcend the images used to convey them. Yet to some degree truth is conveyed, as long as one doesn't deceive oneself by taking these metaphors and similes literally. To do so is to discard the pole of eternal hiddenness, causing one to construe the Divine

solely out of one's own limited experience leading to heresy and deception." **Ephrem The Syrian**

4. "The transcendent infinity of God means that there is no analogy or proportionality between finite and infinite. The transcendent Deity or Godhead is not approachable through any kind of analogical reasoning. The infinite God is "incomprehensible" and "inapprehensible", dwelling in "inaccessible light."" **Nicholas of Cusa**

5. "Nothing exists from eternity but God, and God is not the matter or a part of any creature, but only the Maker." **William Ames**

IMMUTABLE

UNCHANGING OVER TIME

"*Thus God, determining to show more abundantly to the heirs of promise the immutability of His counsel, confirmed it by an oath, that by two immutable things, in which it is impossible for God to lie, we might have strong consolation, who have fled for refuge to lay hold of the hope set before us.*"
— *Hebrews 6:17-18 NKJV*

GOD'S IMMUTABILITY can be found in The Trinity. The Father, The Son (The Logos), and The Holy Ghost have always been. As they have always been, so they have remained. Each is a distinct Person while remaining unified as One God. All three Persons remain immutable. Though each is different in their roles for salvation, They nonetheless are all equally God. They are One, Unified God that moves collectively through Their independence. None operates without the Other knowing, for they are all God. It is God Who is the Immutable Source of life. The Father has given us the blessed promises of both Jesus Christ and the Holy Spirit. The Trinity Themselves are life. Jesus Christ offers us the gift of life. The Holy Spirit gives and lives out the gift of life. The Father judges' life. Each Person is equally God, while

Each provides a specific role in life. Though all Three may appear to work independently, They are dependent upon Each Other.

The Father is not God without the Holy Spirit and Jesus Christ. Jesus Christ is not God without the Father and the Holy Spirit. Likewise, the Holy Spirit is not God without the Father and Jesus Christ. All of Them must coexist to be God. To be God means that They have always been and always will be. "Before the mountains were brought forth, Or ever You had formed the earth and the world, Even from everlasting to everlasting, You *are* God" (Psalm 90:2 NKJV).

It is important to recognize that though all Three from the Godhead may do their work differently, Each is God Themselves. They are All-in-One. Each of Them are immutable in their Personhood. Though there may be variety in how Each of Them operates, They are immutable in their mission. God wants none to perish, but all to come to genuine repentance (2 Peter 3:9). God's longing for all to be saved remains immutable. His longing comes from His Nature. God did not make man to destroy Him. Rather, He made man in order that he might live with Him. How God speaks to each of us may vary. Every Christian that has ever existed has a specific and unique way in which they came to know the Lord. This in no way contradicts God's immutability, but rather solidifies His immutability. He longs for us to have a living relationship with Him. God cannot change His desires, but He can provide a variety of ways in which He moves and goes about His business of drawing us to Him.

God has every right to dictate the standards and ways by which He will draw man to Himself. How He goes about doing so is not worth saying "He is not immutable". We should recognize that His motives are always just, holy, and pure. We must understand that God's nature is unchanging because He is complete within Himself. Since God is complete within Himself, He cannot waiver in Who He is. God is both holy and love. God is both merciful and just. These things do not change, nor do the consequences of either accepting God or rejecting God change.

God's immutability is found through His response towards sin and evil. It is also present towards His response to those who walk in righteousness and holiness. God will bring punishment and consequences towards the ungodly and wicked. However, He will reward those who have been made righteous by Christ's Blood. God's mindset towards good and evil does not change. His *response through action* may differ based upon who has sinned. For Christians, He convicts and chastises. For the nonbeliever, He may simply do nothing until the Day of Judgment. Whatever the case may be, God is immutable in His Being, His nature, and in His mindset towards good and evil. ""For I *am* the Lord, I do not change"" (Malachi 3:6 NKJV).

As we gaze upon God's immutability in admiration, let us visualize His unchanging Being in an understandable manner. Let us imagine for a moment that God is a dot that has always been. Nothing exists outside this infinite dot, but everything that begins comes from inside this dot. Everything that occurs is within this dot, but nothing may pass outside this dot. Attributes of God have always been represented within this dot, fully. There is not one attribute of God's that is not present within this dot. As God has always existed, so His attributes have always existed. God creates all that *resides inside Him*, but God does not create something new *to add to Him*. It is not essential. God has always been perfectly complete within Himself. He does not grow outside of Himself or learn something new. He remains immutable in His Being, in His attributes, and in Himself. God cannot change, for that which changes is not God. Perfection is found in immutability because there is a perpetual constant that cannot be adjusted. Consistency resembles perfection, so long as there be holiness, omnibenevolence, justice, sovereignty, and love involved. As God is all these things, and these things are mere resemblances of God, it follows that He is immutable.

Consequences, actions, and responses from God may be said or done differently, but that which is done differently by God is done from the immutability of Himself. God revealed Himself to Moses in a burning bush (Exodus 3) and in other ways throughout the Old Testament, but now God reveals Himself through His Holy Spirit. The *aim* of revealing Himself through both remains immutable, even if the *process* is different. As times change, God does not change. God's methods of drawing Himself to us may differ, but this is not a contradiction of His Nature. What is done by God is perfectly done with the same immutable goal, even though His methods may vary.

To see this as problematic would be to address the average Christian and say, "People can only come to know Christ through the Holy Bible." Though that which comes from God ultimately comes from His immutable Word, we know this mindset is *partially* wrong. The reason for it being partially wrong is because others can *also* come to know Christ in us by our fruits and the way we live (Matthew 7:15-20).

God's Word remains immutable, but it provides many instructions and deeper revelations to us as we journey down the path of holiness. God's Word gives many different virtues for us to seek and possess. His Word shows us the path to holiness, but not every man or woman in the Bible had the same walk, nor the same strengths. "For the gifts and the calling of God *are* irrevocable" (Romans 11:29 NKJV). God gives a variety of gifts and has made each of us different. He did this for the sole purpose of revealing Himself to others through us. Our mission and calling is to reveal the Immutable God, but how it is done may differ.

It is using differences for the main objective of life. Some of us may work in the health care realm. Others may be teachers and businessmen. Whatever the case, we work within the different realms in which we have been placed, but our message and mission remains the same. Likewise, God is the Immutable One. He is the Way of life and the Mission of life. Varieties of how He speaks and uses us are simply an expression of His omnificence. He specifically designed each of us in such a unique way that not one aspect of life on this earth would be the same. We all differ, but as born-again believers we all strive to live out and share the Immutable Message: the Lord Jesus Christ. May our lives reflect Him Who remains constant. For it is in Him we have a promised hope of salvation. "In hope of eternal life which God, Who cannot lie, promised before time began" (Titus 1:2 NKJV).

God will forever remain the same, for He has always been the same. God is God, just like infinity is infinity. Just as one cannot grasp infinity and bring it down, so one cannot do something in an attempt to change God's Nature. It holds true that God is the only Being to remain constant, while everything He creates changes and can be altered. Only the Unchangeable can transform the changeable. "Of old You laid the foundation of the earth, And the heavens *are* the work of Your hands. They will perish, but You will endure; Yes, they will all grow old like a garment; Like a cloak You will change them, And they will be changed. But You *are* the same, And Your years will have no end" (Psalm 102:25-27 NKJV).

God's immutability will last so long as God endures. Since God has forever been immortal, He will forever be immutable. Though what He creates may be modified and changed, His ability to create remains the same. God may bring new and different things into existence, but the power that is used comes from His Immutable Being. God will design a new heaven and new earth (Revelation 21:1), but these will rest in His immutable, impassable Being. That which is changed, made new, or created comes from the Unchangeable Voice of the One Who has always been.

""God *is* not a man, that He should lie, Nor a son of man, that He should repent. Has He said, and will He not do? Or has He spoken, and will He not make it good?"" (Numbers 23:19 NKJV). What God says will be done will in fact be done. God does not waiver and question what He has already declared. Though there are prayers that may be perceived as "changing God's mind", God already knew that those prayers would be made through His foreknowledge. God's willingness to show us in Scripture that prayer "changes" His mind helps reveal to us the power of prayer. If we don't pray, then God's *complete* will in our lives may be missed. For example, one could be a Christian, but lazy when it comes to their prayer life. They never pray bold prayers that would move God to act and to reveal Himself in a mighty way. Instead, that Christian sits back, idling by throughout this life.

When it comes time for that Christian to go to Heaven, Revelation 21:4 (NKJV) tells us that ""God will wipe away every tear from their eyes; there shall be no more death, nor sorrow, nor crying. There shall be no more pain, for the former things have passed away."" Why will there be crying and tears in Heaven? Isn't Heaven supposed to be a blessed place? Indeed, it is. The reason for tears, however, is that all of us (to some degree) will see that which was missed. God will reveal what could have been if we sought His face and prayed more. Though God was gracious and kind to us in this life, He did not do everything He could have or wanted to do. It is because of our selfishness, sin, idleness, and distraction that we were not able to live *fully* into all that God had for us.

God's immutability provides a predestined plan for all who come to repent and accept Jesus Christ as Lord and Savior. God's overall plan, as well as additional blessings that can be received (both in our lives and the lives of others) remains the same. It is due to our negligence that we miss out on all He has for us. God remains immutable, while we remain mutable in this life.

It is never too late to begin again. It is never too late to pray. May God's immutable plan for each of our lives come to fruition before we are called Home. May our hearts be revived and walk in the power of the Holy Spirit. May we seek His still small voice, and may we pray according to the Immutable Spirit within. It is the Holy Spirit's movement that directs our prayers if we have the strength and patience to remain silent in quiet fellowship with Him. It is only the Holy Spirit that can teach us to pray the Father's will. It is only the prayer found within the Father's will that will be forwarded.

May we find time to spend with the Father. For it is in praying to the Immutable God that His immutable predestined plans for our lives may shine forth. We must endure and put forth the effort if we are to see God's hand move upon our lives. We must not tread lightly in this life. Rather, we must endure carefully. For God honors those who strive towards holiness and pray for His immutable will to be done.

"For I am persuaded that neither death nor life, nor angels nor principalities nor powers, nor things present nor things to come, nor height nor depth, nor any other created thing, shall be able to separate us from the love of God which is in Christ Jesus our Lord" (Romans 8:38-39 NKJV). God loves His creation. He loves those made in His image. He longs for that image to be eternally saved, rather than eternally damned. For His love is unchanging. God loves us, and He loves us to the end. While we are still breathing, may we choose this day to serve the Immutable God. He desires to reveal His purposeful plan to each of us. He can be trusted, for it is only He Who has always been, and continues to remain constant.

O saints, let our hearts soar to the heavens with peace in knowing that God is immutable. Let our souls rest under the shadow of His wing as we meditate on the precious truth that "Jesus Christ *is* the same yesterday, today, and forever" (Hebrews 13:8 NKJV). Blessed be the name of our Lord Jesus Christ. Blessed be the God of immutability.

* * *

HEAVENLY FATHER, we thank You for Your immutability. It is in You that all things are brought forth. That which is brought forth may change, but You, O God, never change. You are the same from the infinite past to the infinite future. Nothing constrains You, for You alone are unwavering. When You declare, it is done. No force or power can change Your ways. God, we thank You that You have provided Your infallible Word to us. May we not merely read it, but may we believe it! May we not merely believe it, may we do it. God Almighty, teach us to pray Your immutable will. We long to serve You, Lord. It is only through knowing Your will that we can do Your will. Holy Spirit, flow through the inner chambers of our hearts. Enlighten our minds with deeper revelations of God's Word. May Your immutable love for us, O God, guide us to love others in like fashion. Though we fall, rise us up in Your strength, Holy Spirit. Defeat sin and self within us, in order that we may live for You all the days of our life. In Jesus' name, Amen.

QUOTES FOR MEDITATION

1. "Is it not a source of wondrous strength to know that the God with Whom we have to do changes not? That His attitude toward us now is the same as it was in eternity past and will be in eternity to come?" **A.W. Tozer**
2. "Can anyone be a father without beginning to be one? Yes, one who did not begin his existence. What begins to exist begins to be a father - God the Father did not begin at all. He is Father in the true sense, because He is not a son as well. Just as the Son is son in the true sense, because He is not a father as well." **Gregory of Nazianzus**
3. "Now all the knowledge and wisdom that is in creatures, whether angels or men, is nothing else but a participation of that one eternal, immutable, and increased wisdom of God." **Ralph Cudworth**
4. "In whatsoever manner it be, let me turn to God and become fruitful in good works. Nothing higher exists than to approach God more than other people and from that to extend His glory among humanity. I will place all my confidence in Your eternal goodness, O God! My soul shall

rejoice in Thee, immutable Being. Be my rock, my light, forever my trust." **Ludwig Van Beethoven**

5. "When God calls a man, He does not repent of it. God does not, as many friends do, love one day, and hate another; or as princes, who make their subjects favorites, and afterwards throw them into prison. This is the blessedness of a saint; his condition admits of no alteration. God's call is founded upon His decree, and His decree is immutable. Acts of grace cannot be reversed. God blots out His people's sins, but not their names." **Thomas Watson**

IMMORTAL

LIVING FOREVER, NEVER DYING

"And whoever lives and believes in Me shall never die. Do you believe this?""
— *John 11:26 NKJV*

CHOOSING to repent and believe in Christ draws one into the presence of Him Who cannot die. God's immortality dwells within His aseity. Since God never had a beginning, He therefore will never have an end. It is God alone Who can give immortality to those He creates in His image. Since all things come forth from Him, there is nothing that has come before Him. If that were the case, then that very thing would be "God". God was never made, created, or developed. God cannot be killed because He is the Foundation and Bedrock of life itself. Take away God and we would dissipate. We cannot move without His presence. He is the Being that has always been. There is nothing that transcends the One Who gives life by a single breath and newness of life by His Spirit.

Those who choose to mock God and curse His name are among the foolish. When a person has anger and rage towards God, they simply damn their souls and increase God's wrath on that coming Judgment Day. Those who believe they are higher and mightier than God have never taken time to meditate on who they are before God. Dictators of the worst kind will stand before God and tremble in His presence. Who dares come against the One Who has always been? Who can strike the One Who controls all things? Who can outthink the One Who possesses wisdom in all dimensions? There is no one who can inflict or bruise God. Though Christ died upon the Cross for our sins, He was raised back to life. God's power of immortality was revealed through the Godman of the Lord Jesus Christ. Though Christ came for one specific purpose – to fulfill God's will by dying on the Cross for mankind's sin and providing a way of salvation – God the Father cannot be touched. His stamina is indescribable, and His immortality is infinite.

Look back throughout history, and we can find that there is a beginning to everything. Now, look back and try to find the beginning of God and you will find no such thing. No being is mightier than He Who rules eternity. Though the angel, Michael, could not beat the fallen angel, Lucifer, Lucifer stands no chance against the One Who made Him. "Yet Michael the archangel, in contending with the devil, when he disputed about the body of Moses, dared not bring against him a reviling accusation, but said, "The Lord rebuke you!'" (Jude 1:9 NKJV). Though Lucifer be a mighty foe in the eyes of angels and mankind, God's omnipotence rules high above Satan. Defeating Satan is just as easy for God as destroying man. God extends His omnipotence and operates throughout His entire Being, effortlessly. Not even Lucifer and 10,000 of his greatest demons could wound God, for our God is Thee Almighty. He exhausts nothing in making, creating, doing, or living. He is outside the realm of weariness and tiredness. Our God Who cannot die, cannot lie. He is "the Alpha and the Omega, *the* Beginning and *the* End, the First and the Last"" (Revelation 22:13 NKJV).

God has placed His never-ending beginning in our beginning. He has breathed in us the breath of life. We cannot die once we are created. We become beings of the Infinite Being when the Cross of Christ marks our soul. "For as in Adam all die, even so in Christ all shall be made alive" (1 Corinthians 15:22 NKJV). Choosing Christ is choosing life. Dying to self is desiring help. This help is that which lingers in the presence of the Immortal One. It is a humbling of oneself and seeing what we are not. It then gazes upon Christ and sees Him for Who He is. We are not only saved by Christ's blood; we live by His blood. We cannot die when the Righteous One stands between us and the Father. It is those who refuse Christ's precious atoning sacrifice that will die twice. Though they will still be alive in the after-life, they will be dead. For Hell is the residing place of the damned.

It is an eye-opening thought to view the beginning of man as a never-ending creature. Those in Hell have died a spiritual death, but they continue to live on in that horrific place. Those who live in Christ, however, are immortal beings who continue to live out the trueness and newness of life. Those who pass on into the next life cannot die because it is the undying presence of God that penetrates our spirits and keeps us alive. "Nor can they die anymore, for they are equal to the angels and are sons of God, being sons of the resurrec-tion" (Luke 20:36 NKJV). God's Spirit is the place in which our souls will rest. God can hold onto every soul and give those the gift of immortality who freely chooses Him. Why? Because He is the only true Immortal Who never had a beginning in the past.

God's immortality is different from all other beings. Since He cannot die, He has the power to allow death. Since He forever lives, He can give life. No matter what opposition a libertarian freewill creature has towards God, the Lord cannot be brought down. None of His attributes can fade. None of His Being can be pelted. He simply is that which He is.

The Being that never had a beginning can know all, for He is all. Death cannot be a consideration to Him, for God cannot even kill Himself. This contradiction of thought should help us all to under-stand that God is too big for Himself to bring down. For to even think that God can kill Himself is a logical impossibility (just as making a round square or a married bachelor is). It is literally something that cannot exist or happen because it is not a real thing. God is not able to do that which contradicts His nature. "For of Him and through Him and to Him *are* all things" (Romans 11:36 NKJV). We cannot kill the Source of all that exists. If we did, then nothing would exist. However, this nothing would still be God, for He cannot be consumed; not even by Himself.

When we think of nothing, we think of complete silence and complete darkness. Even if God were to do such a thing, He Himself would be the blackness and stillness. Nothing can exist and cannot exist apart from God. For it is God Himself Who possesses the realm of nothing and can make it into something. God is not nothing Himself, but He rules the dimensions of that realm where there is nothing besides Him. This place of nothing but God is only known by God because it is a part of God. Just as formlessness is nothing for us, it is still something that is true and part of God because He is incorporeal and not bound by parts.

Nothing can truly exist without the Immortal One. Since God cannot die, He is not bound or ruled by any exterior source in the physical, spiritual, or abstract realm. Since death is a contradiction to God's nature, death itself resides in His hand. The opposite of a physical death, however, is God's Word. Though death is clearly seen throughout our physical world, it is the Word of God that is the only source of *true* life on this earth. "Most assuredly, I say to you, if anyone keeps My word he shall never see death"" (John 8:51 NKJV). God's Word was placed upon this world in written form, in order that all may understand the way to eternal life after they die.

Though there is a spiritual death (which is brought about by sin), spiritual life is not only guided by God's Word, but it was made known through God's Son. ""Most assuredly, I say to you, he who believes in Me has everlasting life. I am the bread of life. Your fathers ate the manna in the wilderness, and are dead. This is the bread which comes down from heaven, that one may eat of it and not die. I am the living bread which came down from heaven. If anyone eats of this bread, he will live forever; and the bread that I shall give is My flesh, which I shall give for the life of the world"" (John 6:47-51 NKJV). The God of Immortality sent His Immortal Son. As the Gospels have revealed to us, Christ not only died, but He rose again on the Third Day. Blessed be "our Savior Jesus Christ, *Who* has abolished death and brought life and immortality to light through the gospel" (2 Timothy 1:10 NKJV). Blessed be the God Who cannot die! Blessed be the One Whose Being possesses omnipotence and sovereignty!

God's Immortality is not one of a dictatorship where He outlives and overpowers everyone. Though it is true He is the Infinite Source of power and life, He does so perfectly. His understanding equips Him to utilize all He is to accomplish that which He pleases. His love calls all to Him, but His love also gives men the ability to choose life or death. God did not make us for the purpose of Him being a tyrant over us. Rather, He made us in order that we could dwell with Him and live with Him for all eternity. God made us through love. When God created the spirit and soul of everyone, He did not do so in order to damn. He did so in hopes of us living in His perfection.

Since God is the Being of perfect Immortality, He therefore is the Being of Life itself. To accept His Word and believe in His Son is to choose life rather than death. "Having been born again, not of corruptible seed but incorruptible, through the Word of God which lives and abides forever" (1 Peter 1:23 NKJV), we live on with the promise of Heaven being our home. Not choosing life, however, leads one to Hell. What is Hell? Simply put, it is a continual, living death. One is forever dying, though they are forever living; experiencing and understanding their death for all time in Hell.

Heaven is the continual living of life. This Life is God Himself, and our spirits fuse into His. Though we will operate independently and will have new bodies, we will not have to worry about sin, wickedness, or death. We will be simultaneously part of God's Incorporeality, while maintaining our individuality as we live on in our new, visible bodies. In Heaven, we will live throughout eternity in righteousness, holiness, and perfection. "For we know that if our earthly house, *this* tent, is destroyed, we have a building from God, a house not made with hands, eternal in the heavens. For in this we groan, earnestly desiring to be clothed with our habitation which is from heaven, if indeed, having been clothed, we shall not be found naked. For we who are in *this* tent groan, being burdened, not because we want to be unclothed, but further clothed, that mortality may be swallowed up by life. Now He who has prepared us for this very thing *is* God, Who also has given us the Spirit as a guarantee" (2 Corinthians 5:1-5 NKJV).

When the Immortal Holy Spirit resides in the born-again believer, we have the glorious promise that "we who are alive *and* remain shall be caught up together with them in the clouds to meet the Lord in the air. And thus we shall always be with the Lord" (1 Thessalonians 4:17 NKJV). God's immortality should refresh our broken hearts and revive our spirits. It should give us the joy of knowing that we serve the One and Only God Who cannot be triumphed over.

Let us forever give praise and thanks to Him Who is the Giver of life. Let us forever thank Christ for His propitiation with the Father by dying on the Cross for our sins. It is our Lord Jesus Christ Who rules and lives and reigns forever. It is the Immortal God Who gives ""eternal life to those who by patient continuance in doing good seek for glory, honor, and immortality" (Romans 2:7 NKJV).

May the promised hope of immortality ignite the fire within to live for Him. "Now to the King eternal, immortal, invisible, to God who alone is wise, *be* honor and glory forever and ever. Amen" (1 Timothy 1:17 NKJV).

* * *

HEAVENLY FATHER, the ultimate perfection of immortality dwells within You. There is no being mightier than You, for You alone have created the heavens and the earth. You bring forth that which exists out of nothing. Your Presence moves effortlessly throughout Your Creation. You hold every man's soul and spirit in the palm of Your hand. It is You Who draws men unto You. It is You Who is calling all of us to live forever with You in that blessed place of Heaven. Lord, we lift Your name up with praise and glory! We seek joyful immortality, for joyful immortality is simply residing in Your presence. God

Almighty, we know that none can compete with You. You are the Ultimate Ruler and Authority. You had no beginning, and You will have no end. You cannot die and death is held in Your hands. God, we look forward to that Final Day when justice will be done. May Your name forever be glorified, O God of Immortality. In Jesus' name, Amen.

QUOTES FOR MEDITATION

1. "There is never a beginning, there is never an end, to the inexplicable continuity of this web of God, but always circular power returning into itself." **Ralph Waldo Emerson**

2. "As the soul is the life of the body, so God is the life of the soul. As therefore the body perishes when the soul leaves it, so the soul dies when God departs from it." **Saint Augustine**

3. "God always was, and always is, and always will be. Or rather, God always Is. For Was and Will be are fragments of our time, and of changeable nature, but He is Eternal Being. And this is the Name that He gives to Himself when giving the Oracle to Moses in the Mount. For in Himself He sums up and contains all Being, having neither beginning in the past nor end in the future; like some great Sea of Being, limitless and unbounded, transcending all conception of time and nature, only adumbrated [intimated] by the mind, and that very dimly and scantily." **Gregory of Nazianzus**

4. "How blessed and amazing are God's gifts, dear friends! Life with immortality, splendor with righteousness, truth with confidence, faith with assurance, self-control with holiness!

And all these things are within our comprehension." **Pope Clement I**

5. "We made bad use of immortality, and so ended up dying; Christ made good use of mortality, so that we might end up living." **Saint Augustine**

INSCRUTABLE

❦

IMPOSSIBLE TO INTERPRET OR UNDERSTAND — IN RELATION TO HOW GOD OPERATES

"*For My thoughts are not your thoughts, neither are your ways My ways, declares the Lord. For as the heavens are higher than the earth, so are My ways higher than your ways and My thoughts than your thoughts.*""
— *Isaiah 55:8-9 ESV*

THE WAYS of the Almighty are inscrutable. That which happens throughout life cannot be fully understood by any except the One in Whom all things exist. God's ways are inscrutable to man because man is finite. In comparison to our thoughts and our ability to comprehend, we have but little understanding compared to God. All understanding belongs to our Heavenly Father and exists through Him. Since understanding and wisdom come from the inner Being of the Most High, it is only rational to conclude that His ways are astronomically higher than ours.

To have the capability of understanding how God operates would position us in a similar realm as Him. Though that which happens in our life can sometimes be understood by the Holy Spirit's speaking, we ourselves cannot understand the *fullness* of anything that happens in our lives with just mere human intellect. To put it into perspective: *it is easier for an infant to learn calculus, than it is for us to understand God's inscrutable ways.* It is only when the Holy Spirit moves and quickens our minds to comprehend the Inscrutable One that we enter into the realm of understanding and are guided to the pillars of knowledge and truth.

When reflection of past events suddenly brings us to a knowledge of why something bad or good happened, it is God Who gives us the understanding. What a blessed truth it is to know that nothing happens within our lives that can exist apart from His knowing. It is God Who *allows* all that comes to happen in our lives. No demon can attack us without God's consent. When allowed, there is always a higher understanding that we do not know behind God's omniscience. God's inscrutable ways not only transcend man's understanding, they surpass all spiritual beings. No angel or demon can comprehend God's mind, for in His very mind they exist. There is no scheme or motive of trickery that can be thought of or planned without our omniscient God knowing.

When evil happens in our lives, God has allowed it in order that He may work out a greater good from it. Though it is tough to accept in the present time, it is through reflection in the future that we can *sometimes* become aware of why it happened. Our comfort, however, should always come to us from the knowledge that one day all things will be explained. God Himself will reveal why He allowed certain things in our life to happen. He will show us the greater good that had worked out because of our suffering and pain that He permitted. It is impossible to understand God's inscrutable ways when we are only able to see the present. The death of a teenage son, for example, could lead to his friend becoming inspired and seeking the deeper things of life. In his pursuit, he becomes one of the most godly, impactful men of his day.

Whatever the case may be, we must allow God's presence to be the consolation during tough times, for He is an understanding Father. "Then the LORD said, "I have surely seen the affliction of my people who are in Egypt and have heard their cry because of their taskmasters. I know their sufferings, and I have come down to deliver them out of the hand of the Egyptians and to bring them up out of that land to a good and broad land, a land flowing with milk and honey, to the place of the Canaanites, the Hittites, the Amorites, the Perizzites, the Hivites, and the Jebusites" (Exodus 3:7-8 ESV). God will bring us to that blessed place; free from pain, evil, and heartache. It is in knowing that God knows and is in control that we can swim through these treacherous waters of life with peace and comfort.

When we lack faith in God, we tend to go through a season of being humbled. For who are we to question His ways? Who are we to disagree? "Then Job answered the Lord and said: "Behold, I am of small account; what shall I answer you? I lay my hand on my mouth. I have spoken once, and I will not answer; twice, but I will proceed no further"" (Job 40:3-5 ESV). It is when God rebukes us in our constant murmuring and questioning that we become silenced. We have no right to question the One Who knows all things. We do not deserve to know, even though we will one day know. God does not keep silent for long. He does not refrain from revealing Himself to His children.

God's omniscience brings forth all understanding of all future, past, and present events. Not only does He know all these things, God also knows that which could have or would have happened and the results that would have followed. This provides God the ability to have ways that transcend all understanding, for He operates and understands both the realm of reality, as well as the realm of possibility. Since He knows both realms, His ways cannot be overthrown. For He knows all fixed events, as well as variable events. This should light the fire of trust within us to believe in the God Who truly can do all things. He is the Mighty One Who simply speaks a word, and it comes forth. There is nothing that Thee Almighty cannot do; especially for those who love Him and seek Him diligently (Proverbs 8:17).

If we truly understood God, we would pray more boldly. Not only would we pray more boldly, but we would also pray with a genuine, strong belief. Many prayers lack results because many prayers lack faith. Majority of prayers are spent in saying the "to do" prayers (such as asking a blessing for the food). Little do Christians realize and comprehend the power that is in prayer. Little do we know the God to Whom we pray. If we could pray to God for only two things, it should be an enhanced understanding of Him and for His will to be done. It is through this type of praying that the fruits of all Christian virtues and responsibilities bloom. It is to The Ruler of heaven and earth that we bow our heads and speak. It is only by the Blood of Christ that He hears our prayers. We must know this, and we must start praying more boldly according to His will.

We must allow our times of quiet fellowship and meditation with the Lord to be intimate and free of distraction. If God is willing to listen, can we not set aside all distractions? It is in the place of solitude and quietness that His voice can be heard. May we find Him in our private prayer time. May the Holy Spirit pray the Father's will through us, as we rest in His presence and trust in His power.

We need not have reason behind that which happens to us when it is permitted by the Omniscient God. For He rules all. He knows all. He is all. He allows all. Nothing happens without reason, for God rules all dimensions. It is in Him that we put our trust. May we believe in the God Who watches after His people. Even though terrible times of tribulation and persecution may come, we can trust that God will raise us above our circumstance. He will bring us to a knowledge that surpasses all human intellect. Even if He does not reveal it in this life, we know that in the afterlife we can ask and receive an answer from Him as to why such things happened.

For our time being on this earth, let us pray powerful, bold prayers. Let us believe in the One Who created us. His purposeful plan for our lives is found in and through His perfect Son. Though we do not understand all things, it is in Him we have all things. May we forever allow His inscrutable ways to bring forth the impossible and unthinkable, according to the riches that are found in Jesus Christ.

"Oh, the depth of the riches and wisdom and knowledge of God! How unsearchable are His judgments and how inscrutable His ways! "For who has known the mind of the Lord, or who has been His counselor?" "Or who has given a gift to Him that He might be repaid?"

For from Him and through Him and to Him are all things. To Him be glory forever. Amen" (Romans 11:33-36 ESV).

* * *

HEAVENLY FATHER, we bless Your Holy Name. You are the God Who knows and understands all things. We thank You that Your ways transcend our ways. Your plan is a purposeful one, and we believe You have good plans for those who love and seek You. Lord, we put our confidence in You. Though we do not always understand, we believe because You rule over all. You are the God Who sees all and dictates all. You are the God Who sent Your Son in order that we can have the opportunity of eternal life in Your blessed presence. We thank You, Father, that Your eye sees those of us who are found in Christ as Christ Himself. May honor, glory, and praise forever be Yours! We believe that whatever is to come in our life, that You see it and have allowed it. We know that You are working out a wonderful plan for Your glory. You are fulfilling Your will through our lives, Lord. May our response of what You allow be derived from our inner being where the Holy Spirit dwells. May He give us the confidence and courage to press on. We love You, Father. In Jesus' name, Amen.

QUOTES FOR MEDITATION

1. "God is that, the greater than which cannot be conceived." **Anselm of Canterbury**
2. "God's name is not known; it is wondered at." **Gregory of Nyssa**
3. "Because we cannot know what God is, but only what He is not, we cannot consider how He is but only how He is not." **Thomas Aquinas**
4. "No one has yet discovered or ever shall discover what God is in His nature and essence... we shall, in time to come, 'know as we are known' (I Cor 13:12). But for the present what reaches us is a scant emanation, as it were a small beam from a great light - which means that anyone who 'knew' God or whose 'knowledge' of Him has been attested to in the Bible, has a manifestly more brilliant knowledge than others not equally illuminated. This superiority was reckoned knowledge in the full sense, not because it really was so, but by the contrast of relative strengths." **Gregory of Nazianzus**
5. "Though every thinking being longs for God, the First Cause, it is powerless... to grasp Him. Tired with the

yearning it chafes at the bit and, careless of the cost, it tries a second tack. Either it looks at things visible and makes of these a god - a gross mistake, for what visible thing is more sublime, more godlike, than its observer... - or else it discovers God through the beauty and order of things seen, using sight as a guide to what transcends sight without losing God through the grandeur of what it sees." **Gregory of Nazianzus**

INCOMPREHENSIBLE

NOT ABLE TO BE UNDERSTOOD
— IN RELATION TO GOD'S BEING

"*"an you search out the deep things of God? Can you find out the limits of the Almighty? They are higher than heaven—what can you do? Deeper than Sheol—what can you know? Their measure is longer than the earth And broader than the sea.""*
— *Job 11:7-9 NKJV*

ONE OF THE best words to describe God in this life can be found in the meaning of incomprehensible; namely, "outside". Whatever we can conjure up in our finite brains, God is most definitely outside that very thing. Not only is He wisdom, love, grace, mercy, justice, holy, and perfect, He is outside them. To try and grasp such complexity is a task of impossibility. Simply put, God is an Ineffable and Incomprehensible Being. We must see Him as great as we can with what we have. We must not limit Him to what we can conjure up. Rather, we must trust that He is the Unknown Being Who has allowed part of Himself to be known.

"Clouds and darkness surround Him; Righteousness and justice *are* the foundation of His throne" (Psalm 97:2 NKJV). God is surrounded by both light and darkness. Though darkness cannot stand in the midst of His presence, darkness still resides within the Being of God. God is not the evil that is regarded as darkness. Rather, the darkness that surrounds God is a lack of light. His Being rules both light and darkness. He is the Light, while His Being contains the darkness. Since His Being is what keeps Hell and the Lake of Fire in existence, He Himself can also be found in the darkest cave and the darkest night.

Regarding spiritual matters, darkness is simply the absence of the *presence* of God, though His *Being* still be there. Mankind distorts that which God makes and rules. However, God does not leave the realm where any evil act is, for He cannot. "And no creature is hidden from His sight, but all are naked and exposed to the eyes of Him to Whom we must give account" (Hebrews 4:13 ESV). Though God's Being is not attached to evil acts and thoughts, the evil acts and thoughts that derive from depraved man happen within God's Being. To have something happen within God – without Him being part of that which is done – is both astounding and fascinating. It is incomprehensible.

Though all *happens* within God, not all *is of* God; especially when speaking of sin and evil. God does not associate with these, for He is a Holy God. The wonderment is how that which is opposite of God's character can happen within Him, while His Being remains pure. Not because He is unable to remain pure, but how that which is opposite of God can happen within Him. He can see and understand the evil and sin that is happening, yet it is not of His nature. This is truly a dimension and reality that no human can fathom.

It is comforting to know that nothing impure is *of* God, even though it may be done *within* Him. God remains perfect and holy. We are the ones who spoil God's presence by our own carnality and iniquity. It is that which is not of God that disgusts Him. Just like a virus in the body is to us, so sin is to God when done within His Righteous Being. He can only remain patient and longsuffering for so long. Eventually there comes a point when justice must be done. This is what the Book of Revelation clearly reveals. Redemption and restoration.

There are no limitations to God. How He moves, speaks, and lives is of greater complexity than any of us could hope to understand. God shares His incomprehensibility in a comprehensible way. However, He is not limited to that which He has revealed. His very nature can be seen and felt both within and without. He reveals Himself to the soul, without revealing Himself in sight. Vice versa, He can reveal Who He is within His creation, but He is not limited to that which He has created. For there is a movement and a force by which we know nothing. Even the highest celestial beings do not know *what* God is. They understand that He is their Ruler and Maker. They understand that He is the Holy and Almighty God; but if we were to speak to them and ask, "What is God?", they could not give a sound answer. There is only One Being Who knows Who God is in His entirety, and that is God Himself.

"But God has revealed *them* to us through His Spirit. For the Spirit searches all things, yes, the deep things of God. For what man knows the things of a man except the spirit of the man which is in him? Even so no one knows the things of God except the Spirit of God" (1 Corinthians 2:10-11 NKJV). It is the Holy Spirit that deepens our revelation and understanding of God. Though eternity is not enough time to understand a decimal of His Being, it is nonetheless worth living and striving to understand. To hear the still small voice and whispers of the Holy Spirit; to allow Him to enter our heart and mind and bring us to a place of understanding we did not have before is worth the sacrifice of self.

When we choose to die to self, we are filled with more of God. It is the Holy Spirit that lives within, and it is the Holy Spirit that reveals more of God to us. To allow Him to do so is to eat the Bread of Life and never be full. Though we may drink of the Living Water and be eternally satisfied, this does not stop the thirst for longing to understand more about our Creator. God's Being is infinite. When we become immortal in the life hereafter, it is then when our journey to understand the Incomprehensible Being will have only just begun. Why wait for that day? We must not be content in idling through this life. Rather, we must become fascinated with the One in Whom we belong. It is in *this* life that we should never stop searching for His hidden secrets. To simply wait until Heaven to know God is to drift into cruise control and be complacent with how things are.

Dear friend, this must never be the case with us who are genuinely born-again. God's Being is beyond Being itself. We know not in full to Whom we pray to. We do not know in *full* Who we think of. We have just gained a touch of Who He is. Yes, we pray to the Triune God, the Three in One. Yes, we know each Person of the Trinity, but we have but an atom of an understanding compared to the unending depths of God. We must seek to have the only One Who knows Him live inside us. We must not only seek to have Him living inside us, but we must seek after His wisdom and knowledge of God. We must continually drift from the distractions of this world and seek after the One Who is incomprehensible.

Is there any greater journey? Is there any greater pursuit? To grow and know more about God, yet, coming to a knowledge as if we were just starting? To be constantly in awe and amazement of Who He is, without really knowing in full of Who He is? This is the unending pursuit of life, and it is in this eternal journey where we will grow in the knowledge of God. Even though an infinite amount of knowledge awaits at any given time in our pursuit, we will nonetheless be in awe with each moment of growth.

"So the people stood afar off, but Moses drew near the thick darkness where God *was*" (Exodus 20:21 NKJV). Let us not be drifters, but pursuers. Let us go after the unending, infinite knowledge that awaits us. Let us allow the Spirit to flow through us and breathe newness of life within us. Let us open our hearts and minds to receive all that we can know of our Incomprehensible God. He awaits the ones who seek after Him, diligently. He longs to show us more of Who He is. We must be willing to submit and kneel with all humility, genuineness, and reverence towards the One Who rules all.

There is not an atom outside God's sight. There is not an act or force that He does not know. There is not a place where He does not rule. There is not a thought where He does not dwell. He is the Incomprehensible God that lies within the deepest and richest dimensions. He exists in all warps of time, space, and abstractions. He is that which is, because He is that which is not known in full by any other being.

To exist in realms unknown to man should excite our spirits! Our souls should fly across the waves of purity, as we prepare for ascension into the unknown place and wisdom of The Unknown Known (see my book *The Unknown Known* for a deeper and more comprehensive understanding of God's Form and Being). May His kindness of revealing small truths strengthen us in knowing that this journey of life has just begun. What lies ahead is beyond human comprehension. May it stimulate our minds to know that together we will all learn more of the Incomprehensible Being. We will continually learn more about the One Who breathed life into us. It is He Who continues to show us the path towards holiness. Great and Mighty is He, Who will be incomprehensible for all eternity.

* * *

HEAVENLY FATHER, no soul, spirit, or living thing will ever be able to grasp or obtain a full understanding of Who You are. Lord, You cannot be fully understood, for You are the Infinite Being that transcends eternity itself. There is nothing of You that can be fully understood, Lord. Learning of You will be a continual, never-ending cycle. For Your power, O God, is infinite and Your attributes are ineffable. We will never comprehend You entirely, but we approach each day of growth in You with excitement. You are the Holy Being. It is You, O Lord, to whom the angels sing. You have created all, for You are all and beyond. You live in the realm of the known, as well as the unknown. We know not what we speak, but we know in Whom we speak too. By the Blood of Christ we are made righteous and able to come before the God of the living and the dead. Great are You, Father, and mysterious are Your ways. As we shall forever grow in You, may we forever put our trust in You. We praise You, O Incomprehensible God. In Jesus' name, Amen.

QUOTES FOR MEDITATION

1. "The name of this infinite and inexhaustible depth and ground of all being is God." **Paul Tillich**
2. "A God comprehended is no God." **Gerhard Tersteegen**
3. "We do not know what God is. God Himself does not know what He is because He is not anything. Literally God is not, because He transcends being." **Johannes Scotus Eriugena**
4. "I know by myself how incomprehensible God is, seeing I cannot comprehend the parts of my own being." **Bernard of Clairvaux**
5. "It is completely incomprehensible to us how God can reveal Himself and to some extent make Himself known in created beings: eternity in time, immensity in space, infinity in finite, immutability in change, being in becoming, the all, as it were, in that which is nothing. This mystery cannot be comprehended; it can only be gratefully acknowledged." **Herman Bavinck**

PROVIDENCE

THE PROTECTIVE CARE OF GOD

"*The Lord descended in the cloud and stood with him there, and proclaimed the name of the Lord. The Lord passed before him and proclaimed, 'The Lord, the Lord, a God merciful and gracious, slow to anger, and abounding in steadfast love and faithfulness, keeping steadfast love for thousands, forgiving iniquity and transgression and sin, but who will by no means clear the guilty, visiting the iniquity of the fathers on the children and the children's children, to the third and the fourth generation.'*"
— *Exodus 34:5-7 ESV*

GOD'S PROVIDENCE goes throughout all the earth and maintains that which is according to His plan. Though all things fade and many fall away from Him, He nonetheless calls all to Him. He is merciful and gracious to all that call upon His name with humility and contrition. When a genuine born-again believer is numbered amongst God's people, God will by no means cast them out (John 6:37). God's protective care is seen throughout all the earth. Though man has defiled that which was pure; though "the god of this world has blinded the minds of the unbelievers, to keep them from seeing the light of the gospel of the glory of Christ" (2 Corinthians 4:4 ESV), God continues to speak and move. It is in His providence that both love and justice dwell. It is love that calls all to Him and seeks for those made in His image to make the decision of choosing Him. It is justice done to those who choose to reject God that reveals His willingness to not allow sin to go unpunished. Both are found in this wonderful attribute of God.

"The Lord is my shepherd; I shall not want. He makes me lie down in green pastures. He leads me beside still waters. He restores my soul. He leads me in paths of righteousness for his name's sake. Even though I walk through the valley of the shadow of death, I will fear no evil, for You are with me; Your rod and Your staff, they comfort me. You prepare a table before me in the presence of my enemies; You anoint my head with oil; my cup overflows" (Psalm 23:1-5 ESV). When we are found in God, we are to fear no man. God's providence will protect us until the time He, by His perfect omniscience, chooses to call us Home. Anything that happens in between is directed and allowed solely by Him. Though God's providence protects our life until He calls us Home to be with Him, this does not exclude us from afflictions, persecutions, and troubles.

God's providence is found in protecting us as we strive to fulfill His will on earth. This, of course, does not mean that life will be an easy path. It was Christ Who walked the path of the crucified life. He did nothing but the will of His Father. The Father protected Him from the Pharisees and all those who despised Him until the Father's omniscient mind and sovereignty allowed Christ to be crucified. ""If the world hates you, know that it has hated Me before it hated you"" (John 15:18 ESV). ""Blessed are you when others revile you and perse-cute you and utter all kinds of evil against you falsely on My account"" (Matthew 5:11 ESV). Knowing that persecution is to come in the Christian life should excite us. We must see how blessed we are when the world despises us. For when it despises us, it means that we are no longer conformed to it. Our image is found in Christ. His providence will lead us through this life until we are to spend an eternity with Him.

"Or do you presume on the riches of his kindness and forbearance and patience, not knowing that God's kindness is meant to lead you to repentance?" (Romans 2:4 ESV). There are times in our life when we fall and sin. We will stumble and go off the narrow path. Though Christ is there to guide us back on the path, we will forever live a repentant life while in this life. As we progress through our Christian walk, it is the sanctification process that develops us into more holy, righteous saints of God. This only occurs by the power of the Holy Spirit through the Blood of Jesus Christ. God's providence is what brings forth the opportunity to grow in Him. His protective care dwells within the genuine convert. It is the Holy Spirit that is the living, experiential Person of God Who resides within us when we are genuinely converted.

"For we do not have a high priest Who is unable to sympathize with our weaknesses, but One Who in every respect has been tempted as we are, yet without sin" (Hebrews 4:15 ESV). Our Lord Jesus Christ knows the burdens that we face throughout this life. We serve a God Who is understanding. Christ was tempted in every way but had no association of falling into those temptations. For our Lord and Savior was the only Perfect Person Who walked this earth without sin. He is the only One Who was always in-tune with the Father's will. Christ was perfect before receiving the Holy Spirit. However, there was an additional supernatural power that came when the Holy Spirit descended upon Christ. As the Spirit fell upon Christ, it was at that moment when Christ's ministry began.

God's providence never allows us to walk through this life alone without His help. Though we strive to live for God throughout this life, we cannot walk into His will without His knowledge and guidance. To live for God, apart from God, is impossible. It is only *by* God that we can live *for* God when we *have* God. This can only be done when we have the Holy Spirit.

"Now we have received not the spirit of the world, but the Spirit Who is from God, that we might understand the things freely given us by God" (1 Corinthians 2:12 ESV). It is the Spirit that begins a ministry that will last for all eternity. It is the Holy Spirit that will show us the way and reveal God's plan to each of us. It is the Holy Spirit that will speak to each of us, uniquely. None of us will have the same experience, though all of us will have the same living Spirit of God inside us who are born-again.

God's providence does not expect us to obey and complete His Word on our own. God understands that for us to understand God's Word, we must have the Holy Spirit. The Father knows that if we are to live by the Word, we must have His Spirit living within us. God Almighty knows that His will can only be completed in us by His Spirit. Without the Holy Spirit, nothing can be done for God, since nothing by itself can understand God.

When we have the Holy Spirit dwelling within us, God's providence can be seen both when we are tempted and when we fall into temptation. "No temptation has overtaken you that is not common to man. God is faithful, and He will not let you be tempted beyond your ability, but with the temptation He will also provide the way of escape, that you may be able to endure it" (1 Corinthians 10:13 ESV). When we are tempted, God's protective care provides a way of escape for His children. He seeks to protect us from that which is contrary to Christ. He can do so because of His omniscience, omnipotence, and omnipresence. All work in unison to provide a means of escape. God's goal is to protect those who love Him from sinning. For it is within the heart of a born-again believer to be free of sin. If we do fall into temptation and sin, God lovingly deals with us. Whether it is gossip, lust, anger, envy, slander, violence; whatever the sin we fall into, God will deal with us accordingly.

When we do that which is contrary to God's nature, His providence does not smite us dead. Rather, it chastises and helps us to grow in Him. ""For the Lord disciplines the one He loves, and chastises every son whom He receives"" (Hebrews 12:6 ESV). God's providence is seen through His response towards sin. To deal with us in tough love is to show us that what we have done is not the way. It is God's tough love that helps us grow in Him and apart from sin.

God's protection of His children is not only seen before temptation, it is seen after when we fall short. God's chastisement upon His children shows that He will not let us disobey and drift from Him without repercussion. The way in which He deals with us, however, is done with love and sound reason. He is willing to discipline in order that we may be protected the next time that we are tempted. We will remember the guilt and shame of our sin and the chastisement and conviction that God bestowed upon us. He does not do this through condemnation, but through His providence. It is this attribute that is always in effect and saying, ""This is the way, walk in it"" (Isaiah 30:21 ESV).

As we walk in the way of God's Spirit, we are bound to go through trials and tribulations. However, we can trust that God will neither leave us nor forsake us (Deuteronomy 31:6). God does not permit us to go through that which is difficult to endure without having a reason behind it. Though we may not understand His inscrutable ways until we are in Heaven, we nonetheless know that it is His providence that will protect us, and it is His grace that will keep us. There is nothing that can happen outside His knowledge. Surely, if God gave purpose and meaning to the martyrs of our day before they died, then our problems and circumstances of financial, health, and relational troubles will not be in vain when we are walking in the way of the Lord.

God longs to do a miracle. He longs to reveal His omnipotence and sovereignty within our lives. We, however, must believe in His providence. We must believe that He loves us, despite our flesh thinking at times that He is neglecting us. There is not one man or woman who is promised an easy life. There is not one of us who will not have to go through the wilderness, swim through the flood, and be burned by the fire. These things, however, are minute in comparison to what lies ahead. "For I consider that the sufferings of this present time are not worth comparing with the glory that is to be revealed to us" (Romans 8:18 ESV).

We must believe that God will protect us and see us through our current trials and difficulties. We must be willing to "Bear one another's burdens" (Galatians 6:2 ESV). God's providence will always give us the right people, resources, opportunities, and attitude throughout our trying times. He can bestow upon us a supernatural peace amid adversity. Paul the Apostle went through one of the hardest walks of the Christian faith. He was tormented and tortured. He had friends abandon him. He went to prison and was beaten nearly to the point of death. Paul, who once was Saul, went from having everything in the world's eyes to being nothing but the dust of the ground for Christ.

God can do the exact same for us. Though we do not wish for such things in our fleshly nature, our spiritual desire is to go through anything and everything for God. It is only by God's providence and the Holy Spirit that we can obtain such a mindset as Paul: "Not that I am speaking of being in need, for I have learned in whatever situation I am to be content. I know how to be brought low, and I know how to abound. In any and every circumstance, I have learned the secret of facing plenty and hunger, abundance and need. I can do all things through Him who strengthens me" (Philippians 4:11-13 ESV).

God's providence can protect us from ourselves. We so quickly forget the prior blessings of the Lord. We are so quick to fall into panic, stress, and dismay. When our perfect routine or rhythm is squandered, we tend to become discouraged and defeated. It is God's providence, however, that can protect us from ourselves. We cannot do anything apart from Christ (John 15:5). It is only the Lord Jesus Christ Who protects us from both Hell and self. When times come where we want to end our lives; when we fall into a spiraling depression where we don't see the point of life anymore, it is God's Spirit Who speaks and ignites His Holy flame. It is the Holy Spirit Who will scorch that which is contrary to God and is weighing us down.

God alone can renew and restore to us the ecstasy we once had in the Lord and walking with Him. "Restore to me the joy of Your salvation, and uphold me with a willing spirit" (Psalm 51:12 ESV). Only God can bring forth newness of life and give us contentment in all circumstances. "And my God will supply every need of yours according to His riches in glory in Christ Jesus" (Philippians 4:19 ESV).

God's providence not only saves us from ourselves, but it also keeps us in our salvation. "For by grace you have been saved through faith. And this is not your own doing; it is the gift of God, not a result of works, so that no one may boast" (Ephesians 2:8-9 ESV). We are saved by nothing we have done. We are saved by everything He has done. Once we have been genuinely converted, it is God Who will keep us and sustain us. Through conviction of sin and sanctification from sin, God keeps us protected through Christ's Blood. "What then shall we say to these things? If God is for us, who can be against us? He Who did not spare His own Son but gave Him up for us all, how will He not also with Him graciously give us all things? Who shall bring any charge against God's elect? It is God Who justifies. Who is to condemn? Christ Jesus is the One Who died—more than that, Who was raised—Who is at the right hand of God, Who indeed is interceding for us. Who shall separate us from the love of Christ? Shall tribulation, or distress, or persecution, or famine, or nakedness, or danger, or sword?" (Romans 8:31-35 ESV). As God allows adversity to come, He does not do so in wanting us to drift from Him. Rather, He does so to draw us towards Him.

God searches the land and looks for those who will trust in His providence. God sees His people and longs to use us as a testimony. It is only God's providence that will get us through adversity. It is trusting in His providence that we are able to remain steadfast and endure until the end. As long as we know that there is a higher mission and purpose behind what we are going through, we can remain at peace. For the God Who created all and knows all is the One Who looks down upon earth and sees each individual person He created.

Though all are made in His *image*, not all are His *children*. As God seeks to draw many to Him, it is the Holy Spirit working through His children that He uses to bring others to Him. Sometimes the only way for someone to know and believe in God is through what God allows to happen in our lives. It is the response we allow the Holy Spirit to enact out from within our soul that makes all the difference. It is us refraining from constant human emotions of negativity that draws others in. It is an unbeliever who sees a genuine convert give thanks and praise to the Lord in all things that makes him think twice about the Living God. As Christians peacefully and patiently wait for God to deliver them, it is the perseverance through adversity that God uses to draw the unbeliever to Him.

We have the libertarian freewill to seek God for His assistance and aid during our difficult times. We are not forced into one response or the other. To have the proper response, we must properly understand that God is for us. God is not out to harm us. He only allows harm to happen for a meaningful, eternal purpose. When we have grasped the fact that all things that happen in life are leading towards the fulfillment of His ultimate will, it is easier to get through and press on. For all things will either provide a means of eternal weight or will be burned on the altar. If we allow God to use us for His glory in any manifestation He chooses; if we respond appropriately, through His grace and help, we will lay up treasures that will not perish.

All genuine believers should seek for eternal treasures. Not for selfish gain, but rather the reasoning behind obtaining the eternal treasures. It is the reasoning behind receiving eternal treasures that should compel us to do what is necessary and right. We as born-again believers are not in it for the treasure itself; we are in it for the meaning that it represents. To have eternal treasures laid up in Heaven reveals to us that we allowed God to work through our lives. It reveals that we had faith in Him during our times of success, failures, and tribulations. May the jewel of faith forever enlarge as we journey throughout this life having full trust and belief in God's providence.

"Humble yourselves, therefore, under the mighty hand of God so that at the proper time He may exalt you, casting all your anxieties on Him, because He cares for you" (1 Peter 5:6-7 ESV). God loves and cares for each of us. We must humble ourselves and kneel before the One Who is complete within Himself. God does not need us. Yet, He cares for us. God's providence proves that He is compassionate and loving. God doesn't want our entire life to be made up of trials; though, they are bound to come. He wants to bring us joy amid whatever life throws at us. Whether we are at the mountain top or in the swamp; wherever the place, God is there. He wants us to rely on and trust in Him.

We cannot begin to fathom the number of things He has protected us from; wrong jobs, wrong relationships, and additional temptations that would have led to additional repercussions and consequences. We must know that what happens within our lives is not all that could have happened. God has always been beside us. He has protected us from things of this world and attacks from the enemy that we know nothing about. If He is so willing to do this for us, then that which happens within our lives should give us peace. We can cast our anxieties on Him. We need not carry our burdens alone. God will raise us up, if we will simply humble ourselves and say, "My Heavenly Father is greater than I, and He understands infinitely more than I ever will." When we have the humility to deny ourselves and disregard ourselves as someone to be served and needing to know everything, it is then when the Lord raises up a testimony within us that will ripple across generations to come.

May the words of Moses in Deuteronomy 8:2-10 (ESV), remind us that God has always been and always will be there for us:

""The whole commandment that I command you today you shall be careful to do, that you may live and multiply, and go in and possess the land that the LORD swore to give to your fathers. And you shall remember the whole way that the LORD your God has led you these forty years in the wilderness, that He might humble you, testing you to know what was in your heart, whether you would keep His commandments or not. And He humbled you and let you hunger and fed you with manna, which you did not know, nor did your fathers know, that He might make you know that man does not live by bread alone, but man lives by every word that comes from the mouth of the LORD. Your clothing did not wear out on you and your foot did not swell these forty years. Know then in your heart that, as a man disciplines his son, the LORD your God disciplines you. So you shall keep the commandments of the LORD your God by walking in His ways and by fearing Him. For the LORD your God is bringing you into a good land, a land of brooks of water, of fountains and springs, flowing out in the valleys and hills, a land of wheat and barley, of vines and fig trees and pomegranates, a land of olive trees and honey, a land in which you will eat bread without scarcity, in which you will lack nothing, a land whose stones are iron, and out of whose hills you can dig copper. And you shall eat and be full, and you shall bless the LORD your God for the good land He has given you."

Let us walk in humility and in the fear of the Lord. Let us remember that He has always been near. If we are alive, living and breathing on this day, then He has led us up to this very point. May we take time to reflect upon that which He has helped us through. May we remember that "Every good gift and every perfect gift is from above, coming down from the Father of lights, with Whom there is no variation or shadow due to change" (James 1:17 ESV). May we come to understand that "His Divine power has granted to us all things that pertain to life and godliness, through the knowledge of Him Who called us to His own glory and excellence" (2 Peter 1:3 ESV). It is the God of all "Who began a good work in you" and Who "will bring it to completion at the day of Jesus Christ" (Philippians 1:6 ESV). "Blessed be the God and Father of our Lord Jesus Christ, Who has blessed us in Christ with every spiritual blessing in the heavenly places" (Ephesians 1:3 ESV).

* * *

HEAVENLY FATHER, we thank You for Your providence. Lord, we know that You see us and You love us. You do not wish us harm, Lord. Though You permit that which is difficult and trying to happen, You do so for Your name and Your glory. May we trust and rest in Your providence. Keep us, O Lord, from the enemy. May we not wander into that which contradicts Your Nature or Your Word. Bring forth an enhanced light within us. Illuminate all that You are within us, Holy Spirit. May our faith remain steadfast because of You working in and through us. May we not become discouraged or depressed when adversity comes. Rather, may we open our eyes to Your providence. You have protected us from so much and have blessed us with so much. Thank You, Father, for doing what only You can do. Give us the grace to continue our walk in You. Help us to finish the race You have set before us. Glory be to You, O God of Providence. In Jesus' name, Amen.

QUOTES FOR MEDITATION

1. "There is not one piece of cosmic dust that is outside the scope of God's sovereign providence." **R.C. Sproul**
2. "No more restless uncertainties, no more anxious desires, no more impatience at the place we are in; for it is God Who has placed us there, and Who holds us in His arms. Can we be unsafe where He has placed us?" **Francois Fenelon**
3. "The mystery of God's providence is a most sublime consideration. It is easy to let our reason run away with itself. It is at a loss when it attempts to search into the eternal decrees of election or the entangled mazes and labyrinths in which the Divine providence walks. This knowledge is too wonderful for us. Man can be very confident that God exercises the most accurate providence over him and his affairs. Nothing comes to pass without our Heavenly Father. No evil comes to pass without His permissive providence, and no good without His ordaining providence to His own ends." **Ezekiel Hopkins**
4. "We should not bear it with bad grace if the answer to our prayer is long delayed. Rather, let us, because of this, show

great patience and resignation. For He delays for this reason: that we may offer Him a fitting occasion of honoring us through His Divine Providence." **Saint John Chrysostom**

5. "There are many who say to the Lord, "I give myself wholly to Thee, without any reserve," but there are few who embrace the practice of this abandonment, which consists in receiving with a certain indifference every sort of event, as it happens in conformity with Divine Providence, as well afflictions as consolations, contempt and reproaches as honor and glory." **Saint Francis de Sales**

PREEMINENCE

SURPASSING ALL OTHER THINGS, SUPERIORITY

"*He Who comes from above is above all; he who is of the earth is earthly and speaks of the earth. He Who comes from heaven is above all.*"
— *John 3:31 NKJV*

JESUS CHRIST IS One of the Three Persons in the Trinity, and therefore dwells in the High and Holy place. He was there before "there" was a word describing location. He was that which was before any other form of life existed. To remain immortal and infinite, while never having a beginning, reveals a firm foundation of superiority. There is no greater being or person than God. Nothing can conquer the Unconquerable. Everything that is not known to man is already known by God. The depths of His wisdom are unsearchable, and the peak of His power is unreachable. There is nothing that God cannot do at any given time. He is the Creator of all things. Therefore, He rules over all things. He can do as He commands at any point in time. For Christ "is the image of the invisible God, the firstborn over all creation" (Colossians 1:15 NKJV). It is only by His very existence that all things exist.

To challenge God is to receive a rebuke from God Almighty Himself. Just as Job was confronted by God for his questioning (Job 38-41), so God can question us at any time. For we were not there during the foundations of the earth. We were not there when breath was given to man. We were not there when the stars were placed in the sky. Before we were in our mother's womb, we remained ignorant of all that had happened up to the point of our birth. For we were nothing. We all were an un-existed person at some point. However, God saw us before we were even created or born. He is the One Who knit us together in our mother's womb (Psalm 139:13).

God knew us before anyone else knew us. He saw how our lives would play out. He saw the mistakes we were going to make and the times we would seek Him. He saw our entire life before we were even created by His Omnipotent Hand. This ability for God to have been at the beginning of all things, reveals to us His preeminence in being the only Unbegotten, Uncreated Being.

God's ability to exist only within Himself reveals that He is Life Itself. The fact that God can see all that is to happen before it is done shows that He is the Preeminent God Who dwells and rules in all dimensions and realms. Nothing moves outside His impassability. Nothing thinks beyond His omniscience. Nothing rises above His omnipotence. Nothing dwells deeper than His immanence. God's Being is found in all and through all. "For by Him all things were created that are in heaven and that are on earth, visible and invisible, whether thrones or dominions or principalities or powers. All things were created through Him and for Him. And He is before all things, and in Him all things consist" (Colossians 1:16-17 NKJV). God moves and exists in all, without being fully attached to that very object, thought, or force of movement. To know this is to better understand the might and power of God's preeminence.

We know that "in the beginning God created the heavens and the earth" (Genesis 1:1). Since God was able to create the heavens and earth in the beginning, we know that God was before them. God existed in whatever realm there was before these things were created. This is knowledge that is only known by God. No one else can attempt to go back to the place that was before the beginning of the heavens and the earth. It is only God Who existed there. It is only God Who could have been the Something to whatever dimension of Nothing that was there. It is therefore God's preeminence that can be found in His aseity and solitariness. To need no other being or creation than Himself brings forth a superiority of astronomical proportions. God needs no one to exist or feel happy. It is only God Who is the True, Independent Being. All other things exist for God's glory and are dependent upon other things; though, all things are dependent upon God.

Humans need to be with other humans to build relationships. Plants need water and sunlight. Dogs need food and a loving human. Our planet needs oxygen and carbon dioxide. Birds need insects. All that has begun to exist is dependent upon something else. God, however, needs no such thing as a source of dependency. God is complete within His aseity and solitariness. He is the Source Who meets the needs of all who are dependent.

It is only God Who can provide that which is needed by all other things. If all things were to submit to God, it would give Him no gain; for He already is infinitely superior. God does not become enhanced, but merely receives the recognition and glory that He deserves from His creation when we choose to follow Him. It is to our benefit to worship and follow the Preeminent God. He gains nothing from us. He simply receives that which is already owed to Him: glory, praise, and worship.

God's preeminence has no match. As all other powers are but a strand of a spider web, God's preeminence is like an elephant. When that strand of web tries to tie up and defeat the elephant, the strand is broken and plowed through effortlessly. Just as the strand is futile to the elephant, so exterior powers are futile when compared to God's preeminence. Though God recognizes attempts from man and Satan to overturn His power, their impact upon God is folly. God is not affected by the powers of Hell, nor the wickedness of man. He scoffs and laughs at their putrid consciences.

God squanders all powers just as easily as a tsunami would destroy a paper house. Try to stand before the Power of all powers, and one will face the obliteration of foolish pride and damnation of the soul. It is foolish to contend with the One Who dwells everywhere. He is Superiority Himself. To deny the supremacy of God's preeminence is to fall prey to self-deception and forever be diluted into a false precept.

Since God does not increase in form, nature, or attribute, He neither decreases in form, nature, or attribute. Yet, He has come down to us from His Infinitude. He is forever already infinite. He cannot go beyond what He already is, for He is Superiority Himself. Once we are perfected in Heaven, we will remain finite compared to God's infinitude. We will be finite beings of immortality. We will never be able to surpass God, but we will always dwell both with and within Him. We will dwell in Him for all eternity, but we will constantly be learning and growing in His preeminence. For there is nothing that will ever reach a peak when seeking after God and His infinitude.

To live the life of constant growth and revelation of Who God is should bring forth reverence. To know that we will never fully understand God, reveals His preeminence. He is the Unknown Being Who makes Himself known. He is the God of unlimited supply. We will never catch up to Him. It is only by His grace and mercy that we have the gift of eternal life and the gift of understanding Him more within each given dimension of time and eternity.

Let us remember, therefore, that Jesus Christ "is the head of the body, the church, Who is the beginning, the firstborn from the dead, that in all things He may have the preeminence. For it pleased *the Father that* in Him all the fullness should dwell, and by Him to reconcile all things to Himself, by Him, whether things on earth or things in heaven, having made peace through the blood of His cross. And you, who once were alienated and enemies in your mind by wicked works, yet now He has reconciled in the body of His flesh through death, to present you holy, and blameless, and above reproach in His sight— if indeed you continue in the faith, grounded and steadfast, and are not moved away from the hope of the gospel which you heard, which was preached to every creature under heaven, of which

I, Paul, became a minister."" (Colossians 1:18-23 NKJV). It is only by the Preeminent Father that Jesus Christ was sent so that we might have newness of life. Therefore, let us press on into our Preeminent Father. Let us remain steadfast and persevere towards the promised hope of Heaven. The Inexhaustible God will surely bring energy to our exhausted self. We will not be conquered when the Unconquerable God goes before us and is with us.

May God's preeminence give us the strength to press on. For "If God *is* for us, who *can be* against us?" (Romans 8:31 NKJV).

* * *

HEAVENLY FATHER, You stand beyond the endless peak. You cannot be topped, nor can You be limited. You are the Preeminent God that surpasses all things. There is no being greater than You. O God, You are superior to all, for all things have come into being because of You. Without You, Lord, nothing was made that was made. We thank You, Father, that Your Love was willing to come down to our level, in order that we may partake and share in Your presence and abundance for all eternity. The blessed Truth that our soul will one day be with You is enough. Lord, You know the struggles and burdens we carry. May Your preeminence conquer that which is ungodly within us. May Your preeminence show us the way where there is no way. You are the God Who can do all things at any given time. We trust and believe in You, Father. Show us Your will and lead us to the place that only You can lead us. We ask for Your protection and strength to endure all things. We love You, Preeminent Father. Our faith rests in You. In Jesus' name, Amen.

QUOTES FOR MEDITATION

1. "We should like Nature to go no further; we should like it to be finite, like our mind; but this is to ignore the greatness and majesty of the Author of things." **Gottfried Leibniz**

2. "What art Thou then, my God? What, but the Lord God? For who is Lord but the Lord? or who is God save our God? Most highest, most good, most potent, most omnipotent; most merciful, yet most just; most hidden, yet most present; most beautiful, yet most strong; stable, yet incomprehensible; unchangeable, yet all-changing; never new, never old; all-renewing, and bringing age upon the proud, and they know it not; ever working, ever at rest; still gathering, yet nothing lacking; supporting, filling, and overspreading; creating, nourishing, and maturing; seeking, yet having all things." **Saint Augustine**

3. "As far as we can reach, He Who Is, and God, are the special names of His Essence; and of these especially He Who Is, not only because when He spoke to Moses in the mount, and Moses asked what His Name was, this was what He called Himself, bidding him say to the people 'I Am has sent

me' (Ex. 3:14), but also because we find that this Name is the more strictly appropriate." **Gregory of Nazianzus**

4. "God does not exist. He is being-itself beyond essence and existence. Therefore to argue that God exists is to deny him." **Paul Tillich**

5. "Therefore Lord, not only are you that than which a greater cannot be thought but you are also Something greater than can be thought." **Anselm of Canterbury**

ATEMPORAL

EXISTING WITHOUT TIME;
UNAFFECTED BY TIME; TIMELESS

"*But, beloved, do not forget this one thing, that with the Lord one day is as a thousand years, and a thousand years as one day. The Lord is not slack concerning His promise, as some count slackness, but is longsuffering toward us, not willing that any should perish but that all should come to repentance.*"
— *2 Peter 3:8-9 NKJV*

WHEN A PERSON CREATES SOMETHING, they are outside of it. Since God is the Creator of time itself, He not only exists and dwells within it, but He also lives outside it. Whatever method of metaphysical time there was before time began for us, God was there. God is not only that which is in the physical realm, but also in the timely realm. Since nothing transcends God Himself, God can create that which He wants humans to understand. God created "time" as we know it to help us live accordingly on this earth. The shortness of time should motivate us to do what is required of us in this life. Even when our finite understanding can only comprehend and understand the hours on a clock and years in a lifetime, God's mind transcends to that which is outside of time itself.

The reality of God's Being not being confined by time allows Him to operate within the past, present, and future in perfect unison. The unveiling truth that one day is a thousand years for God and a thousand years as one day reveals that He is not affected by time. His ability to do what is necessary and perfectly within a specific time shows that His foreknowledge has already been to the place in which we know to be "the future".

Let us imagine for a moment that a man sits upon a mountaintop. From there, he can see all there is in front of him and around him. This is God's relation to time. From a single stance, all of time is seen by God. He sees the moment of Christ's crucifixion at the same time He sees Christ's return. He sits in perfect peace and harmony within Himself because time itself comes from within Himself. Though time comes from within God, He sees outside of it. He sees within the realm He created, but He is not bound by what He has created.

Just as a rushing river goes from one stream to the next, so God's foreknowledge travels across this river of time. We may be represented as separate streams, going from one segment of time to the next, but God is the rushing flow of water that is continually connected to time. He is the water entirely. Therefore, He already understands the future because He is already present there. This magnificent truth is possible only because God is atemporal. Only God is atemporal because He created time Himself. It is a universal truth to know that those who create have both understanding and power outside of that which is created.

Let us look at the life of a woman gardener. She not only starts the garden through planting the seeds and watering them, she herself also has the power to destroy the garden if she so desires. As time progresses, she can pick off the vegetables that the garden has produced. Likewise, God can both make time and destroy time when He so chooses. In regard to eternity in the afterlife, time will be no more for the believer. For the unbeliever, however, time will continue in Hell. To feel every second of time throughout all of eternity will be part of the *torment* of those who have neglected to acknowledge Jesus Christ as Lord and Savior.

Now, just as the gardener can pick the vegetables that have grown from the garden that she has planted, so God is able to pick and choose the placement of Himself within a specific part of time that He Himself created. Though He sees all of time at the same time, He Himself makes Himself partake within certain parts of time. He does this to be present and experience the appropriate emotions within each circumstance. He felt the immense heartbreak of forsaking His Son upon the Cross (Matthew 27:46). He felt vengeance and anger towards Sodom and Gomorrah (Genesis 19:23-29). He felt the tender compassion towards Peter when he tells Jesus that he loves Him (John 21:15-17). He became stern towards Job's questioning (Job 38). He felt betrayed when David committed adultery and murder (2 Samuel 11-12). God can place Himself within time and experience the present moment, in order that the emotions of that event may be felt and experienced in full.

God being atemporal and outside time allows Him to know the perfect plan for man. "A man's heart plans his way, But the LORD directs his steps" (Proverbs 16:9 NKJV). When understanding is met with the heart's intent, it is then able to believe in the atemporal God. It truly begins to believe that God knows what is best. God's timing is perfect because He has created time itself. His ruling of time allows Him to know all that will happen within the given realm of time. He can open opportunities, move upon hearts, and perform miracles at any given time.

Since God is outside time, bringing forth a personal, financial, or wide-based miracle is no challenge. Since He has provided us with the concept of time, He is able to move throughout this life and be present everywhere, at all times. He casts His plays like a master chessman vs. a young child. Effortlessly, He rules the playing field of time since He has created the board of time. As man progresses and learns through innovation, God awaits us to catch up with our future selves. Though God may be with us when we are twenty, He is with us already when we are sixty. The dimension in which He operates projects Him to the place where we have not been and where we have yet to learn and experience. For "That which is has already been, And what is to be has already been" (Ecclesiastes 3:15 NKJV).

How incredible it is to know that if we dedicate our hearts to the Lord, He will establish our ways (Proverbs 16:3). God's omniscience sees all the possibilities that come through each person's libertarian freewill, while already having established a perfect plan regarding any given instance. If a new convert is set on seeking the Lord for the next thirty years of their life, God could raise them up to be the next Billy Graham. If a spouse becomes a drug addict and money that was intended for school tuition for the kids is now being used towards recovery programs, God can work out a financial blessing for those kids to still go to school. Maybe a Christian does one of the most stupid, vile things known to man and is placed in jail. God can take that person and use them to witness and share the Gospel to those who have been sentenced to life in prison. No matter what our foolish, finite, Adam-rooted selves do, God is still able to work out a plan and purpose. He can do so because He has seen every circumstance and has orchestrated the best plan within that given time, place, and event. We may drift ourselves from God's perfect "A plan", but that does not mean God cannot renew and restore meaning and purpose within our lives.

No matter the evil, heartache, and pain that is to come, God has already seen it. He has allowed it in our lives to work out a greater testimony within us. "My times *are* in Your hand; Deliver me from the hand of my enemies, And from those who persecute me" (Psalm 31:15 NKJV). We can receive supernatural peace and joy from God when it comes from a genuine, heartfelt prayer. The very reaction and experience of the Supernatural transcends us beyond the normal human response. Those around will be in awe and shock at the Presence of Him Who dwells within. They will be amazed at how we are not affected by the pains, persecutions, and sufferings of this world. It is then when questions arise, and we can point them to the only Firm Foundation: Almighty God.

""I will never leave you nor forsake you"" (Hebrews 13:5 NKJV). ""I am with you always, even to the end of the age"'" (Matthew 28:20 NKJV). When we believe in the atemporal God, our hearts are suddenly brought into His presence. We are destined to dwell in the realm where the Holy One resides. It is only by the blood of Christ that we have access to the Father. It is only the Triune God Who rules time itself. There is no greater sustainer than the One that not even time can bind.

"Do not boast about tomorrow, For you do not know what a day may bring forth" (Proverbs 27:1 NKJV). May our petty plans be plucked by the roots in order that we may put complete trust in the Holy Spirit to move us towards that which must be done for the day. We are not a people who should worry about the future. Rather, we should live in the present. As God is timeless, we can trust that His omniscience and omnibenevolence will guide us down the path of holiness. When we die to human inclinations, we can live in and for the atemporal God. As genuine converts, it is the timeless Spirit of God that resides within these time-bound bodies.

When the genuine believer passes into the next life, it is our soul and spirit that will ascend to the Heavenly realm. We will be unified *in spirit* with God Himself for all eternity, while independently moving throughout His Being with our new bodies. His Spirit will be an unending current that brings forth eternal jubilation. This over-flowing happiness shall come from His providence and omnibenevolence.

When our soul's dwell within the atemporal God in Heaven, there will be no evil, sin, or demon from Hell that can touch us. No notion of that which is opposite of God will cross paths within our mind. For our mind will be eternally infused with His presence. We will suffer no more pain or persecution, for God's peace will forever surround us. The truth of Heaven should motivate us to purify our conscience and find our renewal of strength in God alone.

"He has made everything beautiful in its time. Also He has put eternity in their hearts, except that no one can find out the work that God does from beginning to end" (Ecclesiastes 3:11 NKJV). The moment God creates a human, they become a being of eternity. Not one of us will ever disappear or dwindle away. Eternity is the charged source within us that never dies. Our residency depends upon our libertarian freewill acceptance or rejection of God. For those in Hell, they will constantly relive the past with no hope of the future. For those in Heaven, they will forever have a future and will have no recognition of the past. Great is this contradiction and mighty is the abundance of wisdom, knowledge, and understanding of God that is to come for those whose souls will be numbered in Heaven.

Let God's transcendence of time give us hope in the recognition and faith that He both knows all and sees all. Let us trust in the atemporal God Who rules over all that is. His wisdom travels with His timelessness. Wherever our atemporal God is, there is where His wisdom and omniscience are found. He rules over all because He sees and knows all. Though demons make estimations of the future, God knows the future, absolutely and infallibly.

As we await our future, may we seek to find God in the now. For as we seek God now, we will see more of Him in the days to come. He is calling us not only to a deeper relationship with Him, but to travel through time with Him. May our minds meditate on the God Who dwells both in and outside time. May we find Him in that blessed, timeless place of prayer. May our souls be destined to dwell in the infinite sea of eternity, in order that we may rest in His perfect love, grace, goodness, and holiness.

* * *

HEAVENLY FATHER, You are the Atemporal God that transcends time itself. We marvel at Your Being. We kneel in admiration before You, the Timeless One. O God, our heart and soul longs for all of You. Lord, we want You to possess and have all of us. What a wonderful day that will be as each tick of eternity passes in Heaven. Every passing moment we will have just begun to know You. Great is the mystery of Your timeless-ness and how wonderful is the knowledge of Your infinite power! As time dwindles and fades within this life, we know that our soul is bound for Heaven to soar like eagles upon still waters. To feel the breeze and touch of Your presence continually will be the satisfaction of our souls. O Heavenly Father, we long to be taken to that timeless place. As eternity has been ascribed upon our hearts, we await Your voice. Help us to do what You have called us to do in this vapor of time, Lord. We long to live for You, the One and Only Atemporal God. In Jesus' name, Amen.

QUOTES FOR MEDITATION

1. "If time came before me, time is not before the Word, whose Begetter is atemporal. When the beginningless Father was there, leaving nothing superior to His Divinity, then also was there the Father's Son, having in the Father a timeless beginning, like the sun's great circle of overwhelming clear light." **Gregory of Nazianzus**
2. "God is outside time not as a frozen, immoveable instant that can do less than us. Rather, He is something Metaphysically bigger than us Whose present encompasses all of our world and time." **Eleanor Stump**
3. "And from true lordship it follows that the true God is living, intelligent, and powerful; from the other perfections, that He is supreme, or supremely perfect. He is eternal and infinite, omnipotent and omniscient; that is, He endures from eternity to eternity; and He is present from infinity to infinity; He rules all things, and He knows all things that happen or can happen." **Isaac Newton**
4. "Time is to eternity as an image is to its exemplar, and those things which are temporal bear a resemblance to those things which are eternal." **Nicholas of Cusa**

5. "Since God is uncreated, He is not Himself affected by that succession of consecutive changes we call time. God dwells in eternity but time dwells in God. He has already lived all our tomorrows as He has lived all our yesterdays." **A.W. Tozer**

ASEITY

SELF-EXISTENT

"*In the beginning was the Word, and the Word was with God, and the Word was God. He was in the beginning with God. All things were made through Him, and without Him nothing was made that was made.*"
— *John 1:1-3 NKJV*

IN THE BEGINNING GOD WAS. He has always been and always will be. God will forever be God so long as God exists. Nothing will ever surpass God and God will never need anything other than God Himself. The God of Heaven and earth is the Preserver of all things. There is nothing that is, that is not within or attached to His Being. As the animals move through the earth, as humans interact through speech, and as the waves rush against the shore, all operate within the realm of God Himself. Nothing can operate without God, for God is in everything, while remaining entirely independent from all things. Only God can be God. Nothing else will comprehend Him fully. Nothing can become more powerful. Nothing will ever surpass Him. God is God, and therefore He is self-existent.

Let us imagine for a moment a snow globe. Let us view all of life within that snow globe. All of earth, all the heavens, all of the universe, and all of time fits within this snow globe. Now, let us view God as the snow globe itself. God is the border to which all that goes on within the snow globe operates; however, that is not all. As we ourselves look at the snow globe, God is also "us" who look at the snow globe. Not only is everything that operates within Him, He is also outside of it, watching from a distance. He is near, yet far. God has no boundaries, no angles in which He must operate. Just as all space, time, matter, and energy exist within Him, God also is as free moving as He is Himself. This means that though God's Being may be the snow globe and all we know in this life exists within the snow globe, God's freedom and existence extends far beyond our understanding.

There is no space in which He cannot touch and does not have access to. There is no area unreached that God has not already visited and been. For all of space is within Him. To meditate on this reality will astound the mind and give understanding that there is only One Who is self-existent within Himself: God Almighty.

""For I *am* the LORD, I do not change"" (Malachi 3:6 NKJV). A being that is self-existent forever remains. God's aseity has always been. "To be" is simply to exist without change. There is no becoming or change. There is no "once was". God's aseity has always been concrete within the foundations of Himself. It is impossible for God to change because change would mean a wavering within Himself. It would mean that His attributes would alternate just as the bars of volume can be seen and displayed on a screen.

God's attributes are like a flat line that we see in the hospital. God always was. Therefore, He will always be. Nothing can enter and fluctuate His attributes. Not even God Himself can change His attributes, for in Him He exists. He relies on no external source. Rather, He Himself is the Source in which He operates, moves, and has His Being.

"Jesus said to them, "Most assuredly, I say to you, before Abraham was, I AM"" (John 8:58 NKJV). Before Abraham was, Christ had always been. As the Father, Son, and Holy Ghost are the Trinity – being All in One – this reveals that Christ never had a beginning, since He Himself is God. Christ finds His sufficiency within God the Father, though He Himself is also God. Great is the mystery of God when reflected and meditated upon. No mind can reach the depths or fully grasp the insurmountable attributes of our Heavenly Father. As our finite minds comprehend that everything had a beginning, they all had a beginning because of the aseity of God. Within His aseity, God can create within Himself that which He has already predestined through His omniscience.

God knows what He will create and reveal within any given time. This ability to already know what is known only by God provides Him the capability to always operate within the boundaries of His aseity; which, in fact, has no boundaries at all. God Himself cannot pass Himself. He is what is. He creates that which has been created. Only One thing has existed in eternity past and that is God Himself. He is the Source of life, love, and hope for all mankind. He is the Creator of all things. He is that worth striving towards because it is He Who placed within the soul of every man and woman the longing fulfillment to be with His Creator: The Almighty God of Aseity.

God is already at the peak of satisfaction within His aseity. The satisfaction and contentment that God finds is found in Him and Him alone. "Nor is He worshiped with men's hands, as though He needed anything, since He gives to all life, breath, and all things" (Acts 17:25 NKJV). God needs nothing from us. We are simply the ones that benefit from His choosing to create us. God in the eternity past was perfectly pleased with Himself in His solitariness. There was nothing He needed. If God had chosen to remain in the state of what was before the creation of the universe, His contentment would be the same as it is now. We are the only beings on this earth that have the libertarian freewill to choose to accept or reject God. It is all for our gain to know Him. As He is a Father of good gifts (Matthew 7:11), He has already presented us with the greatest gift of all: The atoning sacrifice of the Lord Jesus Christ.

Through the great gift of accepting Christ as Lord and Savior, we are opened into a deeper intimacy and experience of knowing God Himself. We exist within His aseity, and we will forever live in Heaven and be surrounded by His presence. Christ's light will be the sun that shines upon the Heavenly realm. We will forever grow with greater joy and deeper revelations of Who God is. This glorious truth should electrify the soul with longing to seek as much of God as we can now.

If God is accessible when we become born-again believers; if a stronger bond can be established by drawing nigh to Him, then why would we wait to know God more and more each day? May distractions and temptations cease from drifting us from God Almighty. Since we now know the Father through the Blood of Christ, it is time to understand that we are in God. ""A little while longer and the world will see Me no more, but you will see Me. Because I live, you will live also. At that day you will know that I *am* in My Father, and you in Me, and I in you. He who has My commandments and keeps them, it is he who loves Me. And he who loves Me will be loved by My Father, and I will love him and manifest Myself to him"" (John 14:19-21 NKJV).

As we walk throughout this world, we can see God and experience Him; not just externally, but internally. The Holy Spirit is the One Who speaks to our soul and draws us into a relationship with the Father. We can walk this earth knowing that nothing can operate outside of God. We can rest in the assurance that *"there is* one God, the Father, of whom *are* all things, and we for Him; and one Lord Jesus Christ, through whom *are* all things, and through whom we *live"* (1 Corinthians 8:6 NKJV).

Let us live for the Prince of Peace. Let us operate within God's aseity. Let us do that which pleases God as we make our way throughout this world which resides in Him. God is not blind to the ways of man. Therefore, may our speech, actions, motives, and deeds be done solely for the purpose of glorifying the King of kings.

Let us rejoice that we are given the opportunity to serve the God of aseity now in this life. He has blessed us with the opportunity to store up riches and glories for the life to come. This is done through the act of seeking and doing His will to further His Kingdom.

Let us rejoice in the God of Aseity! Let us always remember that "of Him and through Him and to Him *are* all things, to Whom *be* glory forever. Amen" (Romans 11:36 NKJV).

* * *

GOD IN HEAVEN, *we give You praise and glory for that which has been given to us. How grateful we are for the life we have, the breath in our lungs, the heart that beats, and the eyes that see. What blessed gifts You have already given to us in this life. God, teach us to pray and seek You in everything we do. Lord, give us greater understanding to know that in You all things exist. You are not controlled, for You control everything. Your Word stands as a firm foundation that cannot be moved. Justice awaits the wicked and blessings await the righteous. Lord, we are nothing in our own strength, but only through the Blood of the One Who always was, always is, and always will be, are we given a purpose and meaning. Glory be to You, Father, for choosing to give us life. You did not have to create us, yet, You chose to. We are thankful that You made each of us different and unique. We praise You for purpose in this life. Like a lighthouse on top of a mountain, may all see the Light of Christ shining within us. May the Holy Spirit flow through us, in order that we may be Christlike to others. Be exalted forevermore, O God of Aseity. In Jesus' name, Amen.*

QUOTES FOR MEDITATION

1. "God not only created the world, initially; but He also preserves it in being." **William Lane Craig**
2. "When we think of anything that has origin we are not thinking of God. God is self-existent, while all created things necessarily originated somewhere at some time. Aside from God, nothing is self-caused." **A.W. Tozer**
3. "Yet how He eludes us! For He is everywhere while He is nowhere, for "where" has to do with matter and space, and God is independent of both. He is unaffected by time or motion, is wholly self-dependent and owes nothing to the worlds His hands have made." **A.W. Tozer**
4. "An idol is anything put in the place of God as the Ultimate Reality – the Eternal, Self-Existent, Uncaused Cause of everything else." **Nancy Pearcey**
5. "A necessary being is a being who cannot not be. It exists by the sheer necessity of its eternal being, of its *aseity*. A self-existent being is not hypothetical or dependent on another concept; it's necessary. God can't not be. Not only is God's being necessary ontologically, but it's also logically

necessary. If anything exists now, something must have *aseity*. God must have the power of being within Himself that is not derived from something outside of Himself. This is transcendent being." **R.C. Sproul**

SOLITARINESS

❧

HAVING LIVED ALONE & ALWAYS EXISTED

"*Hear, O Israel: The Lord our God, the Lord is one!*"
— *Deuteronomy 6:4 NKJV*

THE LORD JESUS CHRIST is the One Who was before the beginning of all things. When there was no such thing as space, earth, and the heavens, God dwelled within Himself. He was His comfort and He needed nothing but Himself. The understanding of God needing no one else but Himself alone can be known as His solitariness. There was no other source of energy, no other voice that needed to be heard. God alone was all He needed, and God alone is continually all He Himself needs.

The Lord does not operate based upon other things. Rather, other things operate based upon God. It is God Who has always been and has always existed. The Lord needs no additions or attachments, for He Himself is entirely complete within Himself. The Lord is not in *need* of worship from others, for He Himself is fully glorified by Himself. It is only to our benefit that we choose to partake in the blessed glory of worshiping our Heavenly Father. The Lord seeks for those made in His image to partake in the worshiping of Him, but He does not need it.

""Remember the former things of old, For I *am* God, and *there is* no other; *I am* God, and *there is* none like Me"" (Isaiah 46:9 NKJV). There is none like the Lord Jesus Christ. He is the only God to be God, and He is the only God to have always been. It is in God's very nature that everything lives, moves, and has its being (Acts 17:28). God Himself is the Author of Life itself. When He was alone in His solitariness, perfect harmony existed. His uninterrupted nature of being simply God provided perfect peace and contentment. This is the blessed place that is only known to God. For God is the only Being to have never not been. God is the only One Who knows what it was truly like to exist solely by Himself. There is no other being that has or will experience this contentment within oneself that is solely apart from all else. It is only God that can express this unique attribute. Though His Being be shared with that which He has created, He Himself needs not that which He has created. God is the same now as He will be in the future. God is the same in the future as He was before the creation of the heavens and the earth.

"For You *are* great, and do wondrous things; You alone *are* God" (Psalm 86:10 NKJV). God alone is God Himself. Everything that God is has always been. God needs no charge of energy, for He is the One Who produces energy. God needs no spiritual realm to reside in, for He Himself is the Infinite Realm. God needs no instruction on how to operate, for He is the Instruction Himself. God simply is That which Is and nothing exists apart from Him.

It is in the inner chambers of God where the unknown secrecies of His Being can be found; though, they may never be fully known. Just as God exists in the heaven of heavens (1 Kings 8:27), so He is the heaven of heavens. He dwells in unknown dimensions and realms. There is no being that can fully fathom or understand the One Who has always been. To exist within Oneself is a mystery we cannot fathom. To have been in a place where there was no place brings forth a sense of awe and fascination. Before all that was came to be, God had lived in that "place" where there was no space, matter, energy, or time. God was neither seen nor heard within that unbegotten "place". God was something that surpassed all realms and dimensions. Though He is spiritual, He is invisible. His presence dwelled within His Being. It was here where there was neither a sound nor feeling that existed beyond God.

It was in the uncreated beginning that the Unbegotten Being dwelled. This place where neither cherubim nor angelic beings of celestial dimensions existed. God had dwelled in that which was Nothing and, at the same time, Everything. Though God be Everything, He dwelled in that realm that was made up of Nothing. Our Heavenly Father dwelled perfectly within His simple, yet Intricate Being. For God is simple in form and complex in being. He will forever remain Ineffable to all beings and things created. For it is only God Who fully understands His *Ineffable Attributes*. It is only God Who knows completely what that Ineffable place of solitariness was and continues to be for Him alone. For that realm which goes beyond all still exists, otherwise God would not exist.

God must dwell in some infinite dimension that is apart from all other things. Otherwise, we would be completely equal to God. Though Heaven is a wonderful place of Christ's presence, that is not *all* of God. Rather, it is *completely* God. For just as a math equation can be *complete*, that equation is not *all* of math. Likewise, for us to understand all of God and to exist in that place where He alone dwells would make us exactly like Him. Though we were made in God's image and given a mind, soul, and spirit, we are not an ineffable being. For there is only one Ineffable Being, which we know only to be God.

We are completely *made* by God without being *entirely* like Him. As born-again believers we are *found in* God, without *being* all of God; even though we have all of God *accessible*. For to have God is to have all of God, without understanding or seeing all of Him. "'Indeed these *are* the mere edges of His ways, And how small a whisper we hear of Him! But the thunder of His power who can understand?'" (Job 26:14 NKJV).

O let us hear the words of Paul the Apostle in Acts 17:23-31

(NKJV), as he addresses Areopagus. What beautiful truths and understanding can be found in this passage:

""For as I was passing through and considering the objects of your worship, I even found an altar with this inscription: TO THE UNKNOWN GOD. Therefore, the One whom you worship without knowing, Him I proclaim to you: God, who made the world and everything in it, since He is Lord of heaven and earth, does not dwell in temples made with hands. Nor is He worshiped with men's hands, as though He needed anything, since He gives to all life, breath, and all things. And He has made from one blood every nation of men to dwell on all the face of the earth, and has determined their preappointed times and the boundaries of their dwellings, so that they should seek the Lord, in the hope that they might grope for Him and find Him, though He is not far from each one of us; for in Him we live and move and have our being, as also some of your own poets have said, 'For we are also His offspring.' Therefore, since we are the offspring of God, we ought not to think that the Divine Nature is like gold or silver or stone, something shaped by art and man's devising. Truly, these times of ignorance God overlooked, but now commands all men everywhere to repent, because He has appointed a day on which He will judge the world in righteousness by the Man whom He has ordained. He has given assurance of this to all by raising Him from the dead.""

God's solitariness is so profound that not even the combined intellect of all beings, angels, and man can fully comprehend its meaning. We can only understand up to the second layer of God's attributes, though an infinite number of layers remain to be sought after and understood. We can comprehend the first layer of His attributes, when we are found in Christ. It is His loving grace that permits it. It is not until the Holy Spirit speaks, that we are able to receive a deeper understanding by entering the second layer of God's attributes: "But the natural man does not receive the things of the Spirit of God, for they are foolishness to him; nor can he know *them*, because they are spiritually discerned" (1 Corinthians 2:14 NKJV). Only the Spirit can give us deeper revelations about God and His attributes. Without the

Holy Spirit, we cannot venture further into knowing Him Who is The Ineffable God.

Let us remember that "for us *there is* one God, the Father, of Whom *are* all things, and we for Him; and one Lord Jesus Christ, through Whom *are* all things, and through Whom we *live*" (1 Corinthians 8:6 NKJV). Let us remember that "without Him nothing was made that was made" (John 1:3 NKJV). It is only by God that all things exist. God needs nothing from that which He creates, for He is already content and complete within Himself alone. It is only to our benefit that we accept the call and purposes He has for our lives. Through the Blood of Christ and by the Holy Spirit we must walk in the will of the Father. God's solitariness needed nothing else that was apart from Him or created by Him; and yet, His sovereign power brought forth man, knowing full well the redemptive and restorative story that would unfold.

It is only by the atoning sacrifice of Jesus Christ that we can begin to learn more about the One in Whom all things exist. It is only by the Spirit's speaking that we can grow in the knowledge and under-standing of the Ineffable God Who always existed. Glory be to the One Who is self-sustaining and perfectly complete within Himself. It is in His complete solitariness, where all began. This place where God dwelled within God. This place where all things that are something, were once nothing. It is in God's solitariness where all possibilities that could happen were known, and all realities would come to be.

God knew what was to come with man. He knew He did not have to create. By His love and mercy, He has given us the opportunity to live with Him for eternity. May we give thanks to the One Who has always been and Who will always be.

* * *

ALMIGHTY GOD, *how magnificent You are in Your solitariness. You need nothing but Yourself. You are all that You need. You do not seek that which You create to feel complete. It is us who hear the call and drawing of the Holy Spirit and seek You that we may feel complete. Thank You, Father, for this blessed gift of life. It is only by Your love, grace, and mercy that we can grow in knowledge and understanding of Your truths. Lord, continue to magnify Your presence to us and through us. Help us to continually learn and grow in You. O God, what curiosity rules our mind when we think of that "place" where it was only You. What a mysterious thought to meditate upon. O God, You Yourself are Thee Provider and Sustainer. Bring us to that place where all our needs are found in You. Give us the grace to seek nowhere else but You for our hope, comfort and joy. We bless You, Father. In Jesus' name, Amen.*

QUOTES FOR MEDITATION

1. "Out of Thee there was nothing, and Thou did'st rejoice in this blessed solitude; Thou are all sufficient in Thyself, and thou hadst no need of anything out of Thyself, for none can give unto Thee, and it is Thou that givest to all by thine all-powerful Word, that is, by Thy simple will." **Francois Fenelon**
2. "During eternity past, God was alone; self-contained, self-sufficient, self-satisfied; in need of nothing." **A.W. Pink**
3. "God was under no constraint, no obligation, no necessity to create. That He chose to do so was purely a sovereign act on His part, caused by nothing outside Himself, determined by nothing but His own mere good pleasure." **A.W. Pink**
4. "Our efficiency without God's sufficiency is only a deficiency." **Vance Havner**
5. "There is no such thing as solitude, nor anything that can be said to be alone and by itself but God, Who is His own circle, and can subsist by Himself." **Thomas Browne**

PLENITUDE

∽

ABUNDANCE

"For in Him dwells all the fullness of the Godhead bodily; and you are complete in Him, Who is the head of all principality and power."
— Colossians 2:9-10 NKJV

THE VERY EXISTENCE of life only comes from God Himself. God's plenitude offers the overwhelming abundance of all we can think, see, ask, wonder, do, imagine, or become. All that is possible is found in the abundance of God Almighty and in Him Who created all things. There is no greater conceivable being than the Living, Triune God. Anything that would try to measure up would immediately be dismantled and squandered. Nothing can produce or bring forth that which is something from nothing. There is no being than can take the invisibility of the soul and reveal it in physical form. Even though we can create life through the gift of sex, we ourselves did not create life itself. It is God Who designed all laws, formalities, morals, imaginations, and worthwhile doings to exist. For that which is good, loving, wise, and holy stem from God Who is these very things.

God Himself is our Abundant Father because He controls, sees, and is through all. "For in Him we live and move and have our being, as also some of your own poets have said, 'For we are also His offspring'" (Acts 17:28 NKJV). As we were made in the image of God (not just having physical dominion over the earth, but also being blessed by God with a mind and soul), so we live because of Him. God is the only One Who can give and take. The greatest form of power is not what is seen in the natural, but what is done in the spiritual. Though man may be able to take another life, he himself cannot take that individual's soul.

It is the soul of a man that operates the mind. From there, we are aware that the mind operates the body. God's plenitude should be recognized in both the physical realm and in the spiritual realm. God's plenitude gives man life, and this life is through the soul. Our lives, however, are not complete until we are found in Christ. From there our life becomes an everlasting life. We live by God's plenitude, and we are saved eternally through His Son, the Lord Jesus Christ.

God's plenitude is quintessential to our uniqueness. Variations of personalities and perceptions are impossible without God. It is only by Him that we can think independently from others (even though our thinking is attached to God). It is His plenitude that provides us with the capacity and capability to interact with others, communicate, and think. It is not by our own being and doing, for we have come into existence only because of God. It is only through God that we can be unique from others, live different lives, be given different purposes and visions, and be blessed with unique talents and gifts. For it is in God's plenitude that all wondrous gifts can be found. These gifts can be found in 1 Corinthians 12:4-11 and 1 Corinthians 12:28-31):

"There are diversities of gifts, but the same Spirit. There are differences of ministries, but the same Lord. And there are diversities of activities, but it is the same God who works all in all. But the manifestation of the Spirit is given to each one for the profit *of all:* for to one is given the word of wisdom through the Spirit, to another the word of knowledge through the same Spirit, to another faith by the same Spirit, to another gifts of healings by the same Spirit, to another the working of miracles, to another prophecy, to another discerning of spirits, to another *different* kinds of tongues, to another the interpretation of tongues. But one and the same Spirit works all these things, distributing to each one individually as He wills." (1 Corinthians 12:4-11 NKJV)

"And God has appointed these in the church: first apostles, second prophets, third teachers, after that miracles, then gifts of healings, helps, administrations, varieties of tongues. *Are* all apostles? *Are* all prophets? *Are* all teachers? *Are* all workers of miracles? Do all have gifts of healings? Do all speak with tongues? Do all interpret? But earnestly desire the best gifts. And yet I show you a more excellent way." (1 Corinthians 12:28-31 NKJV)

Each of us are given unique gifts through the same Spirit. That Spirit is the Holy Spirit. It is God's Spirit that operates through His abundance, equipping us with unique, special gifts. These different gifts are used by different people for the same purpose. For it is in God that life exists. It is God Who longs for all things to recognize His abundance. If we do not understand the truth that all things are found in and come from God, then we will fall prey to the false pretense that it is solely us who create. We will believe that our ideas are our own. Though we have the freedom to think independently, that which is found in God's plan is ultimately done by His implanting of ideas into those who are willing to follow and obey Him.

Though we are free to think and live as we like, we will always be given opportunities to glorify God. We have the decision to choose life or death in all situations. For it is God's love and plenitude that allows us to even contradict Him and go our own way. For if God was not complete in Himself, we would be *forced* to do exactly what He always says. It is only through God's plenitude that we can live and think independently of others, while at the same time be influenced by the Holy Spirit for good.

It is the abundance of life and how life itself is lived that is derived from God's plenitude. We are who we are because of how we were created by our Heavenly Father. "So the LORD said to him, "Who has made man's mouth? Or who makes the mute, the deaf, the seeing, or the blind? *Have* not I, the LORD?"" (Exodus 4:11 NKJV). God gives meaning to all things because He has created all things in a manner that He saw was good. Those who are deaf and mute serve a great purpose in God's overall plan. Though we do not understand fully why this may be, we can recognize the strengths and motivations it may bring to others.

Beethoven wrote some of the greatest music while being deaf. Those who cannot hear, take time to learn how to read people's lips. Helen Keller was a blind and deaf author. Many of the things that are deemed as deficiencies, are given by God for a stronger purpose and meaning to life. These things may occur to motivate those who have all their senses functioning properly to work extra hard and do what is necessary. It may show others that they truly have been blessed, even when they do not possess all that comes from the material world. Whatever the case may be, meaning can be found in God's plenitude. For it is meaning that comes from God. It is God Who gives the abundant supply of all things.

"And of His fullness we have all received, and grace for grace. For the law was given through Moses, *but* grace and truth came through Jesus Christ" (John 1:16-17 NKJV). It is only by God's plenitude that we are given the gift of salvation. Not only are we living beings, but we are also beings that can walk into the fullness of life through Jesus Christ. It is His atoning sacrifice that provides the way from the material to the spiritual; from the temporal to the infinite; from time to eternity. Without the abundance of God bringing forth the only way of salvation, we would starve and deteriorate into an eternal abyss. We would have no hope, for we ourselves are the corruption that combats God's plenitude. Though He brings forth meaning, purpose, imagination, and life to all things, we ourselves have distorted His perfect will through our libertarian freewill of choosing to go down our own paths.

It is God's plenitude that brings forth all things, but all things have the capacity and capability to contrast God. It is only by Christ's blood that we are saved. It is only by the Holy Spirit that we can change and live for the Eternal One. Without Christ and the Holy Spirit, all things would still exist in God, while forever being a lost cause. For without God's Holy Spirit compelling us to come and live for God, we would simply stray further and deeper into our sins, not understanding the true meaning of life. Thanks be to God, however, for the revelation of the Trinity.

Let us remember then that ""the earth is the Lord's, and all its fullness"" (1 Corinthians 10:26 NKJV). Let us come to know that Jesus Christ, "Who being the brightness of *His* glory and the express image of His person, and upholding all things by the word of His power, when He had by Himself purged our sins, sat down at the right hand of the Majesty on high, having become so much better than the angels, as He has by inheritance obtained a more excellent name than they" (Hebrews 1:3 NKJV), is the only way of salvation. He alone is salvation found in God's plenitude. It is in the Living God, Who gives life to all things, that the abundance of all the past, present, and future will flow. That which is known and that which is unknown is found in God's plenitude. He is the Mysterious Being that will never be *fully* comprehended, nor *fully* understood.

It is the simple, child-like faith that begins the journey down the path of holiness. It is the man or woman who comes to God with humility that will be illuminated within. They will be given deeper revelations of Who God is through His written Word and by His Holy Spirit. As revelations are made known and become more pronounced, the Light of all truth will reveal that it is by God's plenitude that what is, is because of God. For God holds all things within His Being. He cannot be conquered or defeated, for His plenitude gives Him sovereignty over all. May we bless His Holy Name.

* * *

HEAVENLY FATHER, You are the Provider and Producer of all things. Lord, nothing can operate, live, or move without Your presence. It is your plenitude that brings forth everything that we see and everything that we are. Help us to grow in the knowledge that You are the God of all things and can do all things. You, O God, give life and purpose to that which You make. Though we be confused at times, we know that all that is to come in our lives is done to bring You glory and grow us in our faith. It is You, O Holy Spirit, that reveals these truths to us day by day. May we forever worship You, God. For without You, we would cease to exist. Thank You for the gift of life. Thank You for the gift of eternal salvation through Jesus Christ our Lord and Savior. Blessed be Your Name, O God of Plenitude. In Jesus' name, Amen.

QUOTES FOR MEDITATION

1. "There exists an infinite, eternal Being, subsisting of Himself, Who is one without being alone; for He finds in His own essence relations whence, with the necessary movement of His life, results the absolute plenitude of His perfection and His happiness. A Being unique and complete, God suffices to Himself." **Jean-Baptiste Henri Lacordaire**
2. "Eternal life and the invisible world are only to be sought in God. Only within Him do all spirits dwell. He is an abyss of individuality, the only infinite plenitude." **Karl Wilhelm Friedrich Schlegel**
3. "The Father, Who is Justice, is not without the Son or the Holy Spirit; and the Holy Spirit, Who kindles the heart of the faithful, is not without the Father and the Son; and the Son, Who is the plenitude of fruition, is not without the Father or the Holy Spirit; they are inseparable in Divine Majesty." **Hildegard of Bingen**
4. "It is by the Holy Spirit that we love those who are united to us in Christ. The more plentifully we have received of the Spirit of Christ, the more perfectly we are able to love them: and the more we love them the more we receive the Spirit.

It is clear, however, that since we love them by the Spirit Who is given to us by Jesus, it is Jesus Himself Who loves them in us." **Thomas Merton**

5. "Prayer is naught else but a yearning of soul ... it draws down the great God into the little heart; it drives the hungry soul up to the plenitude of God; it brings together these two lovers, God and the soul, in a wondrous place where they speak much of love." **Mechthild of Magdeburg**

INCORPOREAL

❧

NOT COMPOSED OF MATTER;
HAVING NO MATERIAL EXISTENCE

""*G*od is Spirit, and those who worship Him must worship in spirit and truth.""*
— *John 4:24 NKJV*

OUR SPIRIT IS an extension of the soul, and it is our soul that is attached to God's incorporeality. Spirit, simply put, is invisible life. As God's incorporeality is invisible, He can also create that which is invisible. None of us can see the soul of another. Even though we cannot see the nature of what the soul is, we can see the different personalities that are derived from each soul. It is God's Spirit, then, that is the Source of life. This Source of life is not understood by any because it is invisible. How it can happen or come to be should forever fascinate us.

Life is only brought forth through God's invisibility. The eternal life that is to dwell in the infinitude of God is our very soul (when we are found in the Body of Christ). We must understand that life has no other way of generating or becoming, apart from God's Spirit and His omniparience and omnipotence. We must see that it is the life of the soul which we should strive to understand and allow to be operated entirely by God.

It is a marvelous wonder to realize that God has neither limits nor extensions. God cannot go outside Himself, for He Himself is already "there". It is His omnipresence that reveals He has no material makeup. Though God's very essence is incomprehensible, we do know that it is Spirit (though it is not limited to just Spirit). There is something that extends beyond the human mind. There is a place where no man or woman can understand or travel across. This place resides within God and belongs only to Him.

The only way we can enter the deeper truths of God is through His Spirit. It is the Holy Spirit that illuminates the soul and brings forth deeper revelations of truth. Our worship is not complete unless it is done by the Holy Spirit. For it to be done by the Holy Spirit, we must die to self and seek the inner life. This inner life is nothing mystical, though it does pertain to the spiritual realm. The inner life is simply understanding and dovetailing one's spirit to that of God's. It is within God's incorporeality that He calls our soul to Him. If we do not go towards His calling, we flounder and miss out on the blessing of knowing and experiencing Him.

One of God's commands for us is to worship Him in spirit and truth (John 4:23-24). Many worship sessions are counted by their externality. It is what looms in the heart and what goes on internally, however, that is assessed and understood as true worship. "For the Word of God *is* living and powerful, and sharper than any two-edged sword, piercing even to the division of soul and spirit, and of joints and marrow, and is a discerner of the thoughts and intents of the heart" (Hebrews 4:12 NKJV). God's Word is made alive only through His Spirit, and His Spirit resides within His incomprehensible Being. His very incorporeality is not made up of matter. Rather, it brings forth matter. His Being cannot be seen. However, He creates that which is seen. His nature cannot be charged by any other source, for He is life Himself. It is His incorporeality that brought forth language and made words come into existence and made His Word visible through His Son and The Holy Bible. For His Spirit guided the hearts and minds of men to write His Word (2 Peter 1:21, 2 Timothy 3:16-17).

God's Word Itself is not physical but is incorporeal. ""And the Father Himself, Who sent Me, has testified of Me. You have neither heard His voice at any time, nor seen His form"" (John 5:37 NKJV). Though God's Word is seen within the Holy Bible and is made visible and readable to us, it comes from Him Who has no necessity of composition. It is God's Word that has already predicted the future, for it has seen the future. This future understanding can only occur by God Himself because He exists outside of time. God's incorporeality funnels through all dimensions and transcends all dimensions. His ability to travel through the material, abstract, spiritual, and timely realms bring forth an understanding that no being can comprehend. Since He knows what will happen in the future (since the future resides within His incorporeality), He makes it known to us through His Word.

That which exists outside the material realm must have a Being that exists outside the material realm and other, different realms. Since the spiritual realm was created by God, God's incorporeality "extends" even deeper and further beyond what we know as the spiritual realm. God ineffably transcends any understanding to life that we can conjure up. His very Incorporeal Form ascends to the realm in which no angel may dwell. Though angels dwell within the spiritual realm in which God created, God extends further into a place only known by Him.

This "place" will forever be known only to God, for this "place" was there when only God lived within His solitariness. It is a part of God that not even angels have seen entirely. "No one has seen God at any time. The only begotten Son, Who is in the bosom of the Father, He has declared *Him*" (John 1:18 NKJV). It is this realm of life that goes beyond even Heaven itself, that no man or woman can venture or know. It is beyond the Heaven of heavens. It is the Holy Place of holy places. It is only for Him Who is Holy, Holy, Holy, and it is what we can refer to as, "The Forever Unknown" (see my book, *The Forever Unknown*, for a mind-expanding reality of this ineffable realm).

As we live our lives seeking holiness, we soon will be brought forth into complete holiness. Our complete holiness will be made possible only by God and being covered by the Blood of Christ. Though we will be made completely holy, God is still holier. He is above even the base of holiness, for He Himself is Holy, Holy, Holy. These three utterances of "Holy" found in Revelation 4 reveal that God is in a realm of holiness apart from all else. To exist in this place where not even man or angels may come to visit Him reveals that God's incorporeality extends beyond what an eternity of knowledge could ever come to find.

"If He goes by me, I do not see *Him;* If He moves past, I do not perceive Him" (Job 9:11 NKJV). When the Holy Spirit moves, we know not when He moves. For even though God is everywhere, we cannot see Him. Though God be around us, we cannot touch Him. ""Look, I go forward, but He is not *there,* And backward, but I cannot perceive Him"" (Job 23:8 NKJV). It is only when the Incorporeal One resides supernaturally within us that we can feel His presence. To feel God and experience Him is to partake in His incorporeality. When we choose to follow and worship God in Truth, this is when Truth is enhanced within us. Though the Truth has always been, it is made known through deeper revelations. The longer a believer lives and seeks the face of God, the more intimate the relationship with God shall be. For those who are continually in God's Word shall continually take in more Truths that will expand the soul and spirit to receive more of God.

Though all of us have the same portion of the Holy Spirit, we do not all have the same fruitfulness. When there are seasons and wanderings of neglecting the Holy Spirit, it is His presence that we squander. Those who are in a state of continually seeking after a deeper relationship with the Living God, however, will bear much fruit. They will know deeper truths than when they first began their walk with the Lord. It is God's incorporeality that allows His Spirit to operate and move within a believer. It is God's incorporeality that allows His Spirit to be in all genuine converts.

God is immutable, though His gifts and speaking to our soul differ with everyone. All His variations of speaking and drawing us to Him strive to lead us to submit to Him and His ways. Since God does not require matter for Himself to exist, He therefore is able to operate as He wishes. For it is within His Aseity that His incorporeality is found.

It is God's incorporeality that produces and brings forth that which is of Him. "No one has seen God at any time. If we love one another, God abides in us, and His love has been perfected in us" (1 John 4:12 NKJV). When God comes to dwell inside the temple of a man, He brings that which is of Him. Since the Holy Spirit is One of the Three in the Godhead, then He Himself contains all that God is. When the Holy Spirit dwells within, we begin to love like Christ. This love is supernatural and must be sought after continually.

It is not the love that man knows to be. Rather, it is love that comes from the Heaven of heavens. It is a love that sent Christ to the Cross in order that we may come to know God the Father. It is a love that sinks into the deepest part of our being. It is a love that draws all men to God. This love is part of our Incorporeal God. When we are found in His incorporeality and brought forth to be one of His children, we then possess that which is only of God: The Holy Spirit. "For since the creation of the world His invisible *attributes* are clearly seen, being understood by the things that are made, *even* His eternal power and Godhead, so that they are without excuse" (Romans 1:20 NKJV).

As the Holy Spirit lives in us, we live by Him. As we operate, move, pray, speak, and do good, we ourselves are taken under control by the Holy Spirit. For our ways are not that of God's. What is of God comes from His nature and His incorporeality. As the Holy Spirit begins to flow more fully through us, it is God's *personal* attributes that become enhanced within us. People will begin to see supernatural grace, mercy, faithfulness, wisdom, and love within us. This is made known only by the Holy Spirit within us Who reveals and makes known these attributes to others.

""You shall not make for yourself a carved image—any likeness *of anything* that *is* in heaven above, or that *is* in the earth beneath, or that *is* in the water under the earth; you shall not bow down to them nor serve them" (Exodus 20:4-5 NKJV). God's incorporeality reveals the foolishness of man when they desire to worship man-made images. Those who desire to worship a "god" that they can create lack sense. They do not understand the massive Inexhaustible Being of our Living Incorporeal God. They desire to worship a false idol in exchange for the great riches and glory that are found in the One and Only True God.

As we grow in seeing the greatness and inapprehensible realities of God, we must be willing to have the courage and boldness to show others Who exactly our Holy God is. He is beyond understanding, though He makes Himself understandable. It is the God of Abraham, Isaac, and Jacob Who is calling all to Him. We must be willing to lovingly show others that a "god" created by man is no god at all. We must point them to the Incorporeal God Who is willing to live within the most wretched sinner if they will simply repent and believe that Jesus Christ is Lord and Savior.

Blessed be the Incorporeal God! Blessed be the One Who cannot be fully grasped or understood. It is through Him that life is created and sustained. It is by Him that His attributes are made known. His omnipresence can be found within His incorporeality. As He exists within His immaterial self, it is God alone Who knows all things. He is the Ruler of all dimensions, all space, and all time. He is the Creator of all that has been, is, and will be made.

May we hear the cherubim sing! May we see the cosmos dance, for God is greater than that which is! May we forever give praise to the One Who is Unassailable. For it is God alone Who is Perfect, Pure, Holy, and Incorporeal.

* * *

HEAVENLY FATHER, we thank You that nothing is outside Your reach or sight. You are the Incorporeal One Who cannot die and never becomes exhausted. You, O God, are the Source of all life. May we strive to feel and experience more of Your Spirit within us. Help us not to squander the Holy Spirit. Give us grace and bring us to a place where no man could bring us. As we walk through this life, let our souls grow closer to You. Blessed be You, O Trinity, for revealing to us each day the deeper Truths of Who You are. May our hearts, minds, and souls be filled with You! We stand in awe of Your incorpo-reality. It is You alone Who rules over all. It is You alone in Whom all things should bow down and worship. Thank You, Father, for the gift of Your Holy Spirit. May He continue to lead us to the place where Your will and Your ways will be met and complete. Unconquerable are You, O Incorporeal God. In Jesus' name, Amen.

QUOTES FOR MEDITATION

1. "Concepts create idols of God, of Whom only wonder can tell us anything." **Gregory of Nyssa**
2. "He [Christ] is the image of the invisible God, the firstborn over all creation. For by Him all things were created that are in Heaven and that are on earth, visible and invisible, whether thrones or dominions or principalities or powers. All things were created through Him and for Him." **Paul the Apostle**
3. "When a sunbeam falls on a transparent substance, the substance itself becomes brilliant, and radiates light from itself. So too Spirit bearing souls, illumined by Him, finally become spiritual themselves, and their grace is sent forth to others. From this comes knowledge of the future, understanding of mysteries, apprehension of hidden things, distribution of wonderful gifts, heavenly citizenship, a place in the choir of angels, endless joy in the presence of God, becoming like God." **Saint Basil**
4. "I do not worship matter, I worship the God of matter, Who became matter for my sake and deigned to inhabit matter,

Who worked out my salvation through matter." **John of Damascus**

5. "All we know of an angel is that it is incorporeal, immaterial, and only by comparing it with God-Who is incomparable-can we see that it has some density and body after all, since in reality only God is truly immaterial and incorporeal." **John of Damascus**

FAITHFULNESS

STEADFAST & LOYAL

""Therefore know that the Lord your God, He is God, the faithful God Who keeps covenant and mercy for a thousand generations with those who love Him and keep His commandments;""
— Deuteronomy 7:9 NKJV

ALL THAT HAS EVER BEGUN to exist has proven to be flawed. There is nothing that has been created that has remained steadfast in faithfulness. There is not one human being that has existed on the face of this earth that has experienced perfect faithfulness amongst the brethren. No one remains stable and faithful throughout their time on this earth. We are all fallen and broken. When compared to a magnificent, omnipotent God, we ourselves are but dust. None of us can compare to Him Who remains faithful.

There is nothing that happens to God, but only that which happens from Him. There is nothing that can affect His faithfulness. He is faithful to the end. When the time comes where we are brought into the spiritual realm of eternity, we will see God's faithfulness. Our faith will be fused into His unfailing faithfulness. We will see justice done to the ungodly and we will see how His faithfulness guided us throughout our lives. As our lives are displayed before Heaven, we will see how God silently displayed His faithfulness within our lives. We will see His wisdom of directing His perfect plan within our lives. We will come to see that it was Him Who brought us where we were and pushed us through to the very end. He is our Faithful Heavenly Father, and He is worthy of praise.

"*Through* the LORD's mercies we are not consumed, Because His compassions fail not. *They are* new every morning; Great *is* Your faithfulness" (Lamentations 3:22-23 NKJV). God's faithfulness is displayed through His mercy towards all men and women. God sending Christ to walk this earth of vileness and wickedness and to be crucified upon a Cross shows that God is faithful. He brought forth the magnificent gift of salvation through the only way possible: the crucifixion of His Perfect, Beloved Son. In this loving act, God revealed to mankind His goodness. Jesus Christ carried the weight and took on the full blow of all sin. He did this so that we might come to know our Heavenly Father. It is only Christ Who could have fulfilled the purposes of such a horrific death. Only Christ could walk the road leading up to the Cross. God could not crucify a sinner to save mankind. The Father had to forsake His Perfect Son upon that Cross to provide and offer newness of life to sinners.

God remains steadfast and loyal to His people. "If we confess our sins, He is faithful and just to forgive us *our* sins and to cleanse us from all unrighteousness" (1 John 1:9 NKJV). If we are to be damned, it is due to our selfish and sinful inclinations. If we are to be saved, it is due to Christ's Blood and God's faithfulness. The Lord does not change His mind, for He is immutable. His promises stand true, even when we do not. It is God "Who cannot lie" (Titus 1:2 NKJV). It is "by two immutable things, in which it is impossible for God to lie, we might have strong consolation, who have fled for refuge to lay hold of the hope set before us" (Hebrews 6:18 NKJV). If God's Word said it, then it has both been done and it will be done. We cannot question the One Who remains immutable in faithfulness. We should not doubt the One Who "is faithful, Who will establish you and guard *you* from the evil one" (2 Thessalonians 3:3 NKJV).

It is only by the protection of God's sovereign grace that we can both fight off the enemy and command him to flee. It is the simple profession of the Blood of Christ that makes any demon of Hell shutter. Their time is short. As God's faithfulness is forever, He will protect us to the very end from the enemy. So long as our soul rests in God's hands and is covered by the Blood of Christ, then no man, demon, or evil spirit can strip us of our salvation.

"He shall cover you with His feathers, And under His wings you shall take refuge; His truth *shall be your* shield and buckler" (Psalm 91:4 NKJV). By the truth of the Scriptures God has proven to man His faithfulness. There is not a chapter in the Bible that has proven insufficient. When the Logos descended from Heaven as Jesus Christ onto this earth, every prophecy about Christ's First Coming in the Old Testament came to pass. For it is the Old Testament that validates the New Testament. Without either Testament, we would not be able to fully grasp God's faithfulness. For it is through both the Old and New Testament that Christ can be seen.

How wonderful and comforting it is to know that God's Word proves true. We can read every sentence and believe it. What God has declared, will happen. What God says He will do, He will do. What God is willing to accomplish through us and do in us, He will do in us and through us; but only if our hearts are set upon Him and we desire to distance ourselves from sin. It is our faith that latches onto His faithfulness. It is the intertwining of the two that leads to trust in God and fulfillment in this life. It is not the promises of blessing, but the promises of God's faithfulness that draw us to the place of supernatural strength, peace, and joy.

""God *is* not a man, that He should lie, Nor a son of man, that He should repent. Has He said, and will He not do? Or has He spoken, and will He not make it good?"" (Numbers 23:19 NKJV). Since the Lord does not need to repent to any other; since He is the Sole Beauty of perfected goodness, He possesses absolute faithfulness. Where can God go apart from Himself? For He Himself is in all things. The beauty seen through His goodness comes from His faithfulness. God will forever love His children. God will always provide for us. He vows to protect us. Though all these beautiful aspects of God's faith-fulness are given to the believer, God is still faithful to call unbelievers to Him. He longs to know all those that He made in His image. He wants to have a living relationship with all His creatures. It is God alone "Who desires all men to be saved and to come to the knowledge of the truth" (2 Timothy 2:4 NKJV).

Though evil and pain done to us would tempt us to hate others, God Himself hates no one in this life (regarding their being). There are "six *things* the LORD hates," however; "Yes, seven *are* an abomina-tion to Him: A proud look, A lying tongue, Hands that shed innocent blood, A heart that devises wicked plans, Feet that are swift in running to evil, A false witness *who* speaks lies, And one who sows discord among brethren" (Proverbs 6:16-19 NKJV). God hates evil and despises wickedness; yet, He loves each person He has created to the very end.

God finds no pleasure in the lost. He does not try to damn anyone. Rather, He calls everyone. It is the failed faithfulness of man that combats God's faithfulness. There is no one to blame but us when we pass off into the next life apart from Him. It is only us who send ourselves to the place that will forever drift from His loving, faithful, kind, gentle, holy, pure, and righteous presence. It is "The LORD, the LORD God" Who is "merciful and gracious, longsuffering, and abounding in goodness and truth, keeping mercy for thousands, for-giving iniquity and transgression and sin, by no means clearing *the guilty*, visiting the iniquity of the fathers upon the children and the children's children to the third and the fourth generation"" (Exodus 34:6-7 NKJV).

Those who reject the Father's call will receive the faithfulness of God's justice. God will honor their decision of not wanting to know Him. Therefore, The Lake of Fire is simply the horrific drifting of God's presence. Those who wanted nothing to do with God in this life, will receive the just dessert of their libertarian freewill decision an infinite fold, as they are cast into the dark abyss for all eternity.

When the wicked hurt us, we have nothing to fear. God commands us to ""Be strong and of good courage, do not fear nor be afraid of them; for the LORD your God, He *is* the One Who goes with you. He will not leave you nor forsake you"" (Deuteronomy 31:6 NKJV). Whatever problems or moments of crisis are to come, God is there fighting for us. We need not worry or fear. Anxiety is the illusion that we are to come up with a way to fix something, when faith is believing God has already figured out and conquered the problem that lies before us. Each of us can walk through this life, knowing that "He Who is in you is greater than he who is in the world" (1 John 4:4 NKJV). God's faithfulness falls upon the believer, through the Holy Spirit. When we have truly believed and repented, it is the Holy Spirit that will never leave us nor forsake us.

It is our Heavenly Father that has given us two wonderful gifts that are derived from One Act: The Father has given us Christ Who died for our sins and offered the way of salvation, and He has given us the Holy Spirit to continue our salvation through sanctification, as we progress down the road of holiness. God's faithfulness is seen in His willingness to truly do everything for us. He has done the most important, most magnificent things that we could ever ask or think. We must come back to the realization that if He is willing to do all this for us, then He will continue to be faithful and fight our battles until we are brought forth to His Throne. For if God "did not spare His Own Son, but delivered Him up for us all, how shall He not with Him also freely give us all things?" (Romans 8:32 NKJV). "And the Lord, He *is* the One who goes before you. He will be with you, He will not leave you nor forsake you; do not fear nor be dismayed"" (Deuteronomy 31:8 NKJV).

Let us remember that "If we are faithless, He remains faithful; He cannot deny Himself" (2 Timothy 2:13 NKJV). God will always be faithful. In His Infinite Being dwells riches untold. Beautiful gifts and ultimate purity rest within the foundation of His faithfulness. Nothing may take from or enter this blessed place. It is God alone Who chooses to share this portion and knowledge with others. His written Word is the beginning of knowing His faithfulness. As we enter the gates of Heaven, we shall see a banner written above in Christ's Blood saying, "Faithful is He."

It is God alone Who can do that which goes against human reasoning. Faithfulness needs no logic. Faithfulness simply needs truth. The bedrock of all truth is in our Infallible God. It is Him Who cannot lie or do wrong. Faithfulness and Truth are the attributes that God stands upon. Without these blessed attributes, mankind would be doomed. It is through the Faithfulness of God that we can rest in knowing that He is Good and Kind.

Let us always remember that "God *is* faithful, by Whom you were called into the fellowship of His Son, Jesus Christ our Lord" (1 Corinthians 1:9 NKJV).

* * *

HEAVENLY FATHER, we thank You that You are the foundation of faithfulness. Lord, Your promises stand true. You have proven Yourself faithful time and time again. We are not worthy of Your faithfulness. Who are we to deserve such love and blessed promises? God in Heaven, we deserve nothing. Yet, You give us everything. We thank You for the blessed gifts of the Lord Jesus Christ and the Holy Spirit. May we continue to be led into that supernatural place of trust. May our faith arise and be not of our own. May our faith come from the Heavenly realm in which You dwell. May all we do be because of You. May we move in Your Being, O Lord, with all confidence and assurance that You are with us. Our hearts seek after the faith that moves mountains, takes away sins, sees miracles, and gives eternal praise and glory to You. Lord, You truly are a God that could not be made up. For that which You do contradicts all that man could or ever would think. Great is Your faithfulness, O Lord. We lift You up, O God of Faithfulness. In Jesus' name, Amen.

QUOTES FOR MEDITATION

1. "Our faith is not meant to get us out of a hard place or change our painful condition. Rather, it is meant to reveal God's faithfulness to us in the midst of our dire situation." **David Wilkerson**
2. "The glory of God's faithfulness is that no sin of ours has ever made Him unfaithful." **Charles Spurgeon**
3. "All God's giants have been weak men and women who have gotten hold of God's faithfulness." **Hudson Taylor**
4. "Far above all finite comprehension is the unchanging faithfulness of God. Everything about God is great, vast, incomparable. He never forgets, never fails, never falters, never forfeits His Word." **A.W. Pink**
5. "The faithfulness of God is a datum of sound theology but to the believer it becomes far more than that: it passes through the processes of the understanding and goes on to become nourishing food for the soul." **A.W. Tozer**

LOVE

WILLING TO GO TO ANY LENGTH OR HEIGHT TO REACH & SAVE THOSE WHO ARE LOST

"*So we have come to know and to believe the love that God has for us. God is love, and whoever abides in love abides in God, and God abides in him."*
   — 1 John 4:16 ESV

LOVE IS the greatest attribute any of us can possess, for it is in love that everything else flows. There is no greater love than that which comes from God. It is in Him where perfect love dwells. This love is deeper than any ocean and it expands further than any galaxy. It is the heart of the Father that blesses man to receive His love through His Son, Jesus Christ. "For God so loved the world, that He gave his only Son, that whoever believes in Him should not perish but have eternal life" (John 3:16 ESV). Without Christ, we would not know what true love is, nor would we be able to see the love God has for us. It is in Christ's crucifixion and resurrection where man finds himself to be loved by God.

There is no greater display than the Cross of Jesus Christ. As He sweated blood on The Mount of Olives (Luke 22:44), He saw each one of us. His heart wept for what was to come, but He wept even more for those who would reject the blessed gift of salvation. Christ was fully aware of the torture and torment that was to occur at His crucifixion. Even with knowing all this, He knew that He was to rise again and conquer death itself.

It was Christ's burdened heart for a dying world that kept Him upon the Cross. Surely, our Lord Jesus could have called to the Father for deliverance. ""Do you think that I cannot appeal to My Father, and He will at once send Me more than twelve legions of angels?"" (Matthew 26:53 ESV). It is supreme power to ask of the Father anything and have it be done. Greater still, the power of love was stronger in Christ than the power of deliverance He had accessible. Christ lived in this life to die in order that we might die to self and live. It was the power of love found in Christ that conquered any self-interest. As humility led Christ to do that which could only be fulfilled by His life, it was His love that made Him endure what was to come.

It was God Who came to us through His Son, Jesus Christ, to be battered and bruised, tortured and tormented, mocked and ridiculed, despised and disdained; all for providing a way of salvation for us. The magnitude of this love has no bounds. To make a way where there was no way. Scripture tells us that "it pleased the LORD to bruise Him" (Isaiah 53:10 KJV). It pleased our Heavenly Father to bruise His Son for the sake of providing a way of salvation to all men. What greater love than to allow His One and Only Perfect Son to die for the sins of a lost and perverse people.

O how the wickedness and godlessness of our day continues to increase! We are a sick and repulsive people! Yet, greater is the Lord's love than our wretched selves. For it is the love towards mankind that made the Father send His Son. If we repent and believe that Jesus Christ is Lord and Savior, our sin is cleansed through just one drop of His precious blood!

"But God, being rich in mercy, because of the great love with which He loved us, even when we were dead in our trespasses, made us alive together with Christ—by grace you have been saved—" (Ephesians 2:4-5 ESV). While we were stuck in the pollution of our sin,

God loved us. While we were habitually sinning, Christ died for us. While we were bound for Hell before our birth, God Almighty did that which would echo throughout all eternity. "God shows His love for us in that while we were still sinners, Christ died for us" (Romans 5:8 ESV). Only God loves the unlovable and changes the most damnable. He does not want any to perish and fall short of knowing Him. He chooses to offer and do that which is undeserved to a despairing and reprehensible people.

How great is this love that can be found in God alone! It is God Who moves and reveals His love to us every day. It is Him alone Who can bless us with a touch from Heaven. It is His love that brings comfort through hardships, peace in calamities, happiness in sorrow, warmth in coldness, and intimacy in loneliness. We must allow His love to harbor within us, in order that its ships may sail to others. Our goal must be for all to know the love of Him Who is Gracious and Merciful.

""A new commandment I give to you, that you love one another: just as I have loved you, you also are to love one another"" (John 13:34 ESV). It is in our expression of love that Christ can be seen through every born-again believer. It is a love that dives deeper than the carnal love of today. This Christ-like love is beyond mere affection. It is a love that does what is right, pure, just, holy, gentle, and kind without expecting reciprocation. It loves for the sake of love, and it desires nothing but to show Christ. It moves throughout all believers in different manifestations. It is love that loves the Lord and seeks to obey Him. It is love that wants to help and encourage all in order that they may be touched by the love of God. It is loving the unlovable and uplifting our neighbor above ourselves. It is praying for our enemies and clothing the poor and needy. It is true love that does what is honorable without seeking honor. It is the love of God that makes us do right for the right reasons. It is His love that is willing to accept all who repent and ask for forgiveness of sins, without hesitation. Blessed is the man or woman who comes to understand this true love that cannot be changed or struck down by Hell itself.

""As the Father has loved me, so have I loved you. Abide in My love. If you keep My commandments, you will abide in My love, just as I have kept My Father's commandments and abide in His love. These things I have spoken to you, that My joy may be in you, and that your joy may be full. "This is My commandment, that you love one another as I have loved you. Greater love has no one than this, that someone lay down his life for his friends. You are My friends if you do what I command you. No longer do I call you servants, for the servant does not know what his master is doing; but I have called you friends, for all that I have heard from My Father I have made known to you. You did not choose Me, but I chose you and appointed you that you should go and bear fruit and that your fruit should abide, so that whatever you ask the Father in My name, He may give it to you. These things I command you, so that you will love one another"" (John 15:9-17 ESV). Love brings forth joy and implants humility. God's perfect love helps us to see the virtuous splendor that can be bestowed upon those who open their hearts to God's love. For it is in the softened heart that God places His omnibenevolent love. We may never *fully* understand the Love that dwells within us, since that Love is the Holy Spirit Himself. Nonetheless, we can thank God for His transformative and supernatural love that continually puts up with and sanctifies us who are born-again.

"Through Him we have also obtained access by faith into this grace in which we stand, and we rejoice in hope of the glory of God. Not only that, but we rejoice in our sufferings, knowing that suffering produces endurance, and endurance produces character, and character produces hope, and hope does not put us to shame, because God's love has been poured into our hearts through the Holy Spirit Who has been given to us" (Romans 5:2-5 ESV). It is God's Spirit that resembles love to the believer. For Him to make His home in a deteriorated temple is to love unconditionally. To be willing to patch up and build up a solid foundation within the believer is the love of the Holy Spirit. If He is willing to live and move within this temple that is in need of constant repair, then surely we can live within the world and love the broken, lost, and marginalized. As all of us need constant maintenance, it is love that is willing to build each other up in the faith and lead all to the One Who paid it all.

Blessed be God the Father for sending His Holy Spirit to love us through our sufferings and to give us strength to endure our adversities. It is the love of the Father that shapes the character of a man or woman through the power of His Holy Spirit. As we grow in the faith, we must grow in love. For with greater faith, comes greater love. The longer we walk with the Lord, the more we come to know His love. The more it changes us. The more it shapes us. It is through greater faith when we love the One Who loves us. It is enhanced faith that brings greater hope in the midst of impossibility. To have hope that transcends our circumstances is to love Him Who cannot lie and will not fail us.

How great and magnificent is He Who lives within! How preeminent is the love of Him Who both saves sinners and changes sinners! If we grasp His love on the Cross, we will long to share His love with the lost. When we find God's love in Christ, we open ourselves to the Holy Spirit revealing deeper revelations of His love. It is the Triune God Who is Love. It is the God of Love Who is calling all to Him.

Let us then accept His love with all humility. Let us not sit in quarreling, bitterness, and strife. We must not allow the prince of hatred to prevail over the King of love. Let us not be particular in who we share our love with; for how can we, when God is in us? "Beloved, let us love one another, for love is from God, and whoever loves has been born of God and knows God. Anyone who does not love does not know God, because God is love. In this the love of God was made manifest among us, that God sent His only Son into the world, so that we might live through Him. In this is love, not that we have loved God but that He loved us and sent His Son to be the propitiation for our sins. Beloved, if God so loved us, we also ought to love one another" (1 John 4:7-11 ESV).

How unfamiliar God's love is to this haughty, pompous world. It does not know the things of God. How can it? How unfamiliar God's love is to those who do not know Him. "See what kind of love the Father has given to us, that we should be called children of God; and so we are. The reason why the world does not know us is that it did not know Him" (1 John 3:1 ESV). May the radiance of God's love make the world question why we live the way we live. May all come to see the rushing water of God's love flow throughout our being. We cannot back away from those who need to be loved the most. For it is in loving the person whom our carnal being would hate where God's love can be seen flowing through us.

Our carnal being will always contradict that which is of God. That is why we must press into our Heavenly Father's love. For it is the love of the spiritual that changes the natural. It is supernatural love that softens the hearts of men and women. It is the Infinite Love poured into our finite being that breaks our heart over our sin and leads us to repentance. As one repents, one must weep. For it is in tears where the heart's brokenness is displayed. It is the heart's silent voice that opens its doors to the love of God.

It is in dying to self, that we come to experience God's love in full. "I have been crucified with Christ. It is no longer I who live, but Christ Who lives in me. And the life I now live in the flesh I live by faith in the Son of God, Who loved me and gave Himself for me" (Galatians 2:20 ESV). When we die to ourselves, we can come to a greater knowledge of Christ's love for us. It is when our eyes no longer see us, but gaze upon Him, that our hearts begin to change. It is no longer living for ourselves but seeing what Christ did for us and choosing to live for Him. It is the willingness to surrender all to Him Who possesses all. We could never live without God. We could never do what God longs to do through us without denying ourselves, taking up our cross, and following Christ (Matthew 16:24). It is in complete denial of ourselves that perfect love from the Father may flow in us and through us. So long as we keep Christ at the forefront, we will experience His love with great jubilation.

Let us remember that "Love is patient and kind; love does not envy or boast; it is not arrogant or rude. It does not insist on its own way; it is not irritable or resentful; it does not rejoice at wrongdoing, but rejoices with the truth. Love bears all things, believes all things, hopes all things, endures all things" (1 Corinthians 13:4-7 ESV). Let us keep pressing on, forever knowing that God is "merciful and gracious, slow to anger and abounding in steadfast love and faithfulness" (Psalm 86:15 ESV).

Thanks be to God for His precious Son Who died for our sins in order that we may have eternal life. No greater act of love has been done than that which was done by the Triune God. May our souls prostrate before the One Whose love endured upon the Cross for our sins. Glory be to Him forever! Let us "give thanks to the God of heaven, for His steadfast love endures forever" (Psalm 136:26 ESV).

* * *

HEAVENLY FATHER, we thank You for Your love that has no bounds. Lord, You loved us before we were even born. You loved us before anyone knew us. God, we are humbled by Christ's crucifixion. Lord, we do not deserve Your love. Yet, You give it so freely. May we allow that love to pour over us. May that love be felt and placed within every atom of our body. Lord, our souls thirst for Your love. It is Your love, O Lord, that provides us with hope, changes our character, and leads us to do that which cannot be done in our own strength. Help us to love others, just as You have loved us. How grateful we are to know You, God of Love. In Jesus' name, Amen.

QUOTES FOR MEDITATION

1. "When a man's intellect is constantly with God, his desire grows beyond all measure into an intense longing for God and his incisiveness is completely transformed into divine love. For by continual participation in the Divine radiance his intellect becomes totally filled with light; and when it has reintegrated its passible aspect, it redirects this aspect towards God, filling it with an incomprehensible and intense longing for Him and with unceasing love, thus drawing it entirely away from worldly things to the Divine."
   Maximus the Confessor

2. "Pure love is in the will alone; it is no sentimental love, for the imagination has no part in it; it loves, if we may so express it, without feeling, as faith believes without seeing."
   Francois Fenelon

3. "No matter how low down you are; no matter what your disposition has been; you may be low in your thoughts, words, and actions; you may be selfish; your heart may be overflowing with corruption and wickedness; yet Jesus will have compassion upon you. He will speak comforting words to you; not treat you coldly or spurn you, as perhaps

those of earth would, but will speak tender words, and words of love and affection and kindness. Just come at once. He is a faithful friend - a friend that sticketh closer than a brother." **D.L. Moody**

4. "He [Jesus Christ] loves to see poor sinners coming to Him, He is pleased to see them lie at His feet pleading His promises; and if you thus come to Christ, He will not send you away without His Spirit; no, but will receive and bless you." **George Whitfield**

5. "I have given God countless reasons not to love me. None of them has been strong enough to change Him." **Paul Washer**

GRACE

UNMERITED FAVOR

"*The Lord is merciful and gracious, slow to anger and abounding in steadfast love.*"
— *Psalm 103:8 ESV*

IT IS the blessed attribute of grace that none of us deserve. Grace is God Himself, for it is that which brings forth the new creature within man. As we find ourselves in Christ, it is His grace that continues to change us by the power of the Holy Spirit. God's grace is incomprehensible because it offers to do the very thing that man would not do. It is willing to forgive that which is most contrary to God's nature. It is the grace of God that gives hope to the wretched sinner and soars him into the bosom of Jesus Christ. It is in this place where we find rest in God and God alone. It is through God's grace that we can have hope in a blessed future. This future is one that is personal to each born-again believer, but it has one central theme: Forgiveness of sin as one continues their walk in holiness. So long as we walk with a repentant heart, God is willing to forgive.

It is God's grace that carries us. When we grieve His heart, His grace leads us to sorrow over our sin. There will forever be unlimited grace for the Christian who lives their life in genuine repentance. For it is through repentance that the genuineness of seeking after the things of God is made known. Repentance and obedience are not works of the faith, but attributes of the faith. Those who do them reveal that they truly know Him.

"For the grace of God has appeared, bringing salvation for all people, training us to renounce ungodliness and worldly passions, and to live self-controlled, upright, and godly lives in the present age" (Titus 2:11-12 ESV). It is the grace of God that reveals to us the path of eternal life. Though we are saved at the moment of our conversion, it is God's grace that gives us Heaven now. As Heaven lives in our hearts once we have the Holy Spirit, it is God's grace that gives rest to our souls and peace of mind. Without God's grace, we would be caught up in a life of religion. We would not have the freedom of knowing that we "are no longer a slave, but a son, and if a son, then an heir through God" (Galatians 4:7 ESV). It is God's grace that gives us the awareness that we do not make it to Heaven based upon how we live. For it is "by grace you have been saved through faith. And this is not your own doing; it is the gift of God, not a result of works, so that no one may boast" (Ephesians 2:8-9 ESV).

How blessed are we to know that our salvation is found through the precious blood of Jesus Christ! It is God Who sent His Son to die for us in hopes that we would freely come to Him by the drawing of the Holy Spirit. It is God alone Who longs to save all and is longsuffering. It is our Heavenly Father that longs for no one to perish, and calls all to Him (2 Peter 3:9). "If we confess our sins, He is faithful and just to forgive us our sins and to cleanse us from all unrighteousness" (1 John 1:9 ESV). O how miraculous is this grace! This grace that covers us and overflows. If our hearts are willing to confess our sins and repent, it is He Who will sustain and help us through this life. Though God does not condone sin or allow excuses, He realizes that without His grace we all would likewise perish. It is His grace that transforms us into the saints that He desires us to be!

It is unreasonable in the eyes of man to give grace to another man who has done an abominable, wicked sin. Think of the worst sin imaginable - it is God Who is willing to forgive and cleanse that man! The grace of God is beyond that which is understood by man. The worst of what man can do to us, God is willing to forgive. It is God Who respects no persons, but it is His grace that is freely offered and given to all. How foolish it would be to reject such undeserved grace! What a gift we have through our blessed Savior! It is God alone Who can forgive even the most repulsive sinner. Though men and women may forgive those closest to them, it is the grace of the Holy Spirit working through us that is willing to forgive any who trespass and sin against us.

How great is the grace of God to give His Spirit! For the movement of His grace is within His very Spirit! It is the Holy Spirit Who sanctifies us! The grace of God has sent us the Holy Spirit to turn us wretched sinners into holy saints of God through the blood of Jesus Christ. It is only grace that allows sanctification. It is only sanctification by the Holy Spirit that allows us to change and prepare for eternity. For it is God alone "Who saved us and called us to a holy calling, not because of our works but because of His own purpose and grace, which He gave us in Christ Jesus before the ages began" (2 Timothy 1:9 ESV).

O the vileness and wickedness of those who would seek to distort and pervert the grace of God! O how multitudes have trampled on such a beautiful, undeserved gift. Who could turn the grace of God into lasciviousness (Jude 1:4) once grace has truly been understood? Who could turn and spit in the Lord's face and say, "I don't need You or Your help. I'm quite fine on my own"? Who could live a life that says, "God's grace will always cover me, so I will do as I please. I will just come back after I sin and ask for forgiveness, because He will always be there"? O what perverseness goes on in the world and within the church today! How wrong we have it! To take God's grace and to believe we can use it as an insurance policy for heaven. To think that we can take His very grace and use it as a license to sin. "What shall we say then? Are we to continue in sin that grace may abound? By no means! How can we who died to sin still live in it?"

(Romans 6:1-2 ESV). O how wretched are we who know not the true meaning of God's grace!

God's grace is not merely forgiveness of sin; it is empowerment over sin! God does not merely give us that which we don't deserve, He also gives us what we need in order to conquer the very thing that is contrary to His Nature. It is sin and self that needs to be purged from our being, and it is only the grace of God that can do so! "And rend your hearts and not your garments. Return to the Lord your God, for He is gracious and merciful, slow to anger, and abounding in steadfast love; and He relents over disaster" (Joel 2:13 ESV). When we find ourselves falling into temptation and sinning, it is the grace of God that brings forth life in the midst of death. Though we have done, said, or thought that which offends or angers God, God nevertheless comes forth with arms open wide. He speaks to us and says, "My grace is sufficient for you, for My power is made perfect in weakness"" (2 Corinthians 12:9 ESV).

Never should we shrug our shoulders and say, "I can't change the way I am." Of course you cannot, but God can through His grace and by the power of His Holy Spirit! We must be like Paul and "...boast all the more gladly of (our) weaknesses, so that the power of Christ may rest upon (us)" (2 Corinthians 12:9 ESV). For it is in our weakness that we are made strong. It is in our failures where God shows up in a miraculous way.

It is only God's grace that can take all the credit for a changed character within us. When our weaknesses and old habitual states become temptations not acted upon, it is at this stage when we see that God has helped us. It is God's grace that makes old lifestyles change into ones filled with more righteousness. The scales of sin will always fall when we stop looking to ourselves for help and start looking to God! We can do nothing apart from Christ (John 15:5). No matter how hard we try, we cannot permanently change our way of life without a miraculous touch from the Holy Ghost! It is His grace that is willing to come to us in our darkest hours. It is when we believe we are so lost that God cannot save us that the Light of Grace shines within our soul and says, "You then, My child, be strengthened by the grace that is in Christ Jesus" (2 Timothy 2:1 ESV).

It is only Christ Who saves. It is only God's grace that makes us change. We are finite beings of temporal changes, but God is the Infinite One Who brings forth eternal changes. May His willingness to reach into Hell itself and grab us out give us a realization that He is for us and not against us. He longs to do that which we do not deserve. For it is through this that His perfect love and purity is revealed. No Atheist or Agnostic can bring forth good reasons that God is wicked when His grace is revealed through the Scriptures and seen within our lives.

We must never compare ourselves with others but come to know that "all have sinned and fall short of the glory of God, and are justified by His grace as a gift, through the redemption that is in Christ Jesus" (Romans 3:23-24 ESV). When we as Christians fall into sin, we must "with confidence draw near to the throne of grace, that we may receive mercy and find grace to help in time of need" (Hebrews 4:16 ESV). As we genuinely pursue to walk the Christian Road, we must not fall into depression when we slip into temptation. "For the Lord your God is gracious and merciful and will not turn away His face from you, if you return to Him" (2 Chronicles 30:9b ESV). We must always remember that God's grace longs to forgive and conquer sin within our lives.

It is Satan who seeks to condemn us in our sin, while God convicts us when we sin. The Lord convicts us ever-so lovingly, in order that we may once again repent and cling to His grace. God has the power to defeat sin, but it is us who must access that power through our prayer life. It is in asking God to give us a heart that hates sin and one that fears Him that we will begin to see a supernatural change within us. It is this mindset and prayer that enhances the realm of grace and evidence of its working in our lives.

"For from His fullness we have all received, grace upon grace" (John 1:16). God gives His grace to all people in hopes that they come to know Him. When we are found in Him, He gives us His grace that forgives our daily sins and weaknesses. It is then "grace upon grace" that empowers us born-again believers to find victory in our walk with Him! No longer do addictions and past lifestyles rule our minds and hearts, for these chains have been broken! It is the deepened revelation of Who Christ is and understanding the wickedness of sin that draws us to a place where we seek God's grace more than we ever did before. When we show God that we are serious about our walk, His "grace upon grace" will flow through us. His grace will open the prison doors that we were trapped by for so long. His grace will lead us out of those cells and into the meadows of freedom.

"Therefore, preparing your minds for action, and being sober-minded, set your hope fully on the grace that will be brought to you at the revelation of Jesus Christ" (1 Peter 1:13 ESV). Let us always look to the blessed hope in Jesus Christ. We do not deserve Him. We do not deserve the gift of salvation, but O how we should grab ahold of this blessed gift of His grace! We should cling to His lovingkindness ever-so quickly! Who would be willing to forgive sin after sin after sin? It is only God Who is willing. To give us blessings that we do not deserve should motivate us to properly worship and respect our Heavenly Father. He is the God of Grace, and there is no other. It is only Him Who conquered death, Hades, and Lucifer. It is only God Almighty Who is willing and just to forgive us of our sins and cleanse us from all unrighteousness (1 John 1:9). It is only our Immanent Father Who gives us the Holy Spirit to sanctify us and make us righteous through the blood of Jesus Christ. It is only our Sovereign Lord that empowers us to fight temptations and break old lifestyles and habits. He is the God of Freedom. In Him alone is Life. It is His grace that should encourage us to press on. It is His grace that will cover us by the blood of Christ and keep us written in the Book of Life.

If all this be true, what does it matter that we suffer a little while for the Lord? What does it matter when trials and adversity come? If God is so willing to forgive our deepest, darkest, and most sinful secrets, how much more should we forgive those who do us wrong? We all have silent, hidden sins. We all have acted in ways or said things that we regret. We all have done things that made us lament. When we review our lives in eternity, there will be so much filth and remorse of the things we had done in this life; but thanks be to God that we will be saved! Thanks be to God that we will see continued progress of growing more righteous! Thanks be to the grace of God that He not only is willing to meet us where we are, but He is willing to take us past where we are!

It is only God's grace that grows us towards eternity. It is only God's grace that saves us for all eternity. Blessed be "the God of all grace, Who has called you to His eternal glory in Christ" Who "will Himself restore, confirm, strengthen, and establish you" (1 Peter 5:10 ESV). Blessed be the name of our Lord Jesus Christ!

May "The grace of the Lord Jesus Christ be with your spirit" (Philippians 4:23 ESV). May "the grace of the Lord Jesus Christ and the love of God and the fellowship of the Holy Spirit be with you all" (2 Corinthians 13:14 ESV). May we forever "grow in the grace and knowledge of our Lord and Savior Jesus Christ. To Him be the glory both now and to the day of eternity. Amen" (2 Peter 3:18 ESV).

* * *

HEAVENLY FATHER, we are grateful for Your grace that does not compare to human understanding or reasoning. Lord, You are so willing to give us all things. Your protective care and love for us is beyond comprehension. Why You would look down and be so longsuffering with us is a mystery that can only be learned through Your grace. Though we will never fully understand Your grace, Father, we are grateful for It. Thank You for calling us and changing us into men and women of righteousness. It is by Your continued grace that we will become the holy saints You want us to be. You alone are God, O Lord. You alone can wash us clean by Your precious blood. We praise You and bless You for Your grace that moves us closer to Your heart, Father. May You continue to show us the way. May Your grace overflow within us, in order that we may show the same grace to those around us. In Jesus' name, Amen.

QUOTES FOR MEDITATION

1. "Grace is the good pleasure of God that inclines him to bestow benefits upon the undeserving. It is a self-existent principle inherent in the Divine nature and appears to us as a self-caused propensity to pity the wretched, spare the guilty, welcome the outcast, and bring into favor those who were before under just disapprobation. Its use to us sinful men is to save us and make us sit together in heavenly places to demonstrate to the ages the exceeding riches of God's kindness to us in Christ Jesus." **A.W. Tozer**
2. "Great sins do draw out great grace; and where guilt is most terrible and fierce, there the mercy of God in Christ, when showed to the soul, appears most high and mighty." **John Bunyan**
3. "For God will deign to visit the dwellings of just men -- delighted, and with frequent intercourse -- thither will send his winged messengers on errants of supernal grace." **John Milton**
4. "Man is closer to God according to his existence in grace than he is according to his existence in nature." **Thomas Aquinas**

5. "By His gracious condescension God became man and is called man for the sake of man and by exchanging His condition for ours revealed the power that elevates man to God through his love for God and brings God down to man because of His love for man. By this blessed inversion, man is made God by divinization and God is made man by hominization. For the Word of God and God wills always and in all things to accomplish the mystery of His embodiment." **Maximus the Confessor**

MERCY

⸎

COMPASSION; FORGIVENESS
THAT IS UNDESERVED

"*P*raise be to the God and Father of our Lord Jesus Christ! In His great mercy He has given us new birth into a living hope through the resurrection of Jesus Christ from the dead.*"*
— *1 Peter 1:3 NIV*

WE DO NOT DESERVE God's mercy, yet He gives so, graciously. If we take time to view ourselves, we can rationally conclude that we are not good in and of ourselves. ""There is no one righteous, not even one"" (Romans 3:10 NIV). All of us can look within and realize that we are wicked, internally. We may do the right thing at given times, but is it an attempt to prove to others how "good" we are? Most times when we do good, we give ourselves a pat on the back saying, "well done". If we were to weigh our good deeds against our bad thoughts alone, we would come to realize that we ourselves are not good people. A way of validating this claim is in the following question: If asked, "would it be okay if we took all of your thoughts in the past year and put them on a screen for all to see?", would that be okay with you? If you cringe at the thought, then there is your answer.

Each one of us deserve Hell. If Paul said he was the worst of all sinners (1 Timothy 1:15), I am his captain. I recognize that the natural, carnal, internal being of who I am (apart from Christ) is wicked. Without the LORD Jesus, I am a man filled with envy, rage, jealousy, hate, lust, depression, and hopelessness. Glory be to God, however, that when the Holy Spirit comes, He takes off the scales and gives us new hopes. He brings forth that which comes from above. He ignites His holiness within and leads us down the heavenly path where Christ is. We no longer are the wretched sinners we once were. We are now sinners saved by the blood of the Lord Jesus Christ and made new through the sanctifying work of the Holy Spirit. "He saved us, not because of righteous things we had done, but because of His mercy. He saved us through the washing of rebirth and renewal by the Holy Spirit" (Titus 3:5 NIV). We no longer sink into the swamp of sin, but we climb the mountain of righteousness. Though we may slip on our way up, Christ is there to help us, guide us, and strengthen us.

O what a blessed truth lingers within the chambers of The Unknown; the dwelling place where only God lives! Who can find the depths of the mercy of the Father; the God Who forsook His Own Son on a cross in order that we may live? What parent would place their child as a living sacrifice and provide a way for all murderers, liars, idolaters, adulterers, rapists, and prideful, arrogant men to be saved? Tell me! Who out there would do that which goes beyond human comprehension, in the hope of drawing sinners and the ungodly into a living relationship?

Dear friends, we deserve nothing from God, yet, we have every-thing in Him! He has opened the endless sea of His mercy for us to dive into! Why would we stand at the shore and say "no"? Why would we refuse to repent and turn unto God for salvation through Jesus Christ? God does not look for perfection, but rather a willing heart. It is the progressive walk of a believer that bears fruit, not the self-deceived stagnant that sits in the muck and mire of this world.

Can't we see what God has done? When we are born-again, we do not have to live in our sin; for God has forgiven it (if we come to Him with a genuine heart of repentance and belief in Him). "Praise be to the God and Father of our Lord Jesus Christ, the Father of compassion and the God of all comfort, Who comforts us in all our troubles, so that we can comfort those in any trouble with the comfort we ourselves receive from God" (2 Corinthians 1:3-4 NIV).

It is mind-boggling to think that when we fall short and disobey God, His hand of fury does not smite us right then and there. It is beyond finite understanding that when we have had our worst day, God stays with us. Though there are repercussions and consequences for our sins; though God may at times need to be distant, He does this to reveal to us that His ways are best. He shows us that without Him, we are nothing; but in Him, we are everything. He blesses us with conviction in hopes of turning us back to Him. Sin is a lie and lasts but a short time. It is like a bolt of lighting. It strikes our being with ferocious conviction and consequences.

That which entices and excites us usually is that which we must be blind to. ""And if your eye causes you to sin, tear it out. It is better for you to enter the kingdom of God with one eye than with two eyes to be thrown into hell"" (Mark 9:47 ESV). Christ's warning here is to show us that sin is not worth going to Hell for. It is better to go into Heaven not all in one piece than to be thrown into Hell in one piece. It is the body that deteriorates and dies, but it is the soul that ascends and lives. We must see the delicacy of the soul and spirit that God has given unto us. He longs for us to be drawn to Him in order that His presence may provide the protection needed to further us along into His blessed promises.

"Be merciful, just as your Father is merciful" (Luke 6:36 NIV). We are called to allow God's incomprehensible mercy to flow through us towards all we come in contact. Whether on the job, in our family, on the team, or acquaintances we meet, we must portray the same mercy that God has given and continues to give to us. ""If anyone slaps you on the right cheek, turn to them the other cheek also"" (Matthew 5:39 NIV). If we are persecuted by this world, may they see Christ through our neglect of retaliation. Though our fleshly nature would enjoy saying or doing harm in equal fashion, it takes greater power and courage to resist and be of a gentle spirit. For this mindset to flow, we must have the maturity of possessing a compassionate heart towards the unbeliever.

No matter how annoying or wrong someone may be, we must realize the certainty of the destination that awaits those who don't know Christ. We must feel more pain for the souls that are on the way to being damned in Hell than we do feeling the emotional or physical pain within the given moment. For what awaits them is beyond anything we can fathom. What they do to us is simply a testing of our faith and an opportunity of receiving greater reward in Heaven.

Pain and hardships from others in this world provide the opportunity of a greater testimony of Christ working through our lives. Without Christ, we would not be able to be merciful. With Christ, we are synced into the promises and powers of the supernatural realm. Mercy we never had is now accessible through the Holy Spirit. That which bothered us years ago finds no place in affecting us now. It is all because of our maturing in the wonderful mercy of God.

God is the Eternal One Who possesses eternal forgiveness of sins and salvation to those who seek Him. In God's mercy, He does all He can to operate within the world to draw all to Him. He does not hang sin over us unless it is in loving conviction to draw us to Him. God's love for His creation is seen through His reaction to us believers. "If we confess our sins, He is faithful and just and will forgive us our sins and purify us from all unrighteousness" (1 John 1:9 NIV). How merciful is He, to save us from Hell for all eternity! Though each of us deserve Hell at best, it is the Holy Spirit that helps us put our sins to rest.

How merciful is our Father in Heaven to breathe His Spirit into us. Who would want to dwell in the temple of ex-drunkards, ex-adulterers, ex-murders? Yet, in God's mercy, He frees us from the bondage of sin. He places us in the sea of His mercy, and it is Christ's blood that is the eternal water of this never-ending sea.

O to be drowned in the blood of Christ! To understand the reality that because He died for our sins, we can live in freedom. Though we fall, He is there to pick us up. Though become angry with ourselves for falling, He is there to show us the way once again. His mercy does not keep remembrance of our sins to condemn us. Rather, He whispers them to us when we are about to slip once again. He reminds us of the last time we did that sin and found no long-lasting pleasure or fulfillment. We were empty. We were sad that we had grieved His Spirit.

O may He bestow upon each of us the remembrance of the after-effect of our sins, in order that we may turn immediately from our temptations! ""Watch and pray so that you will not fall into temptation. The spirit is willing, but the flesh is weak"" (Matthew 26:41 NIV). We must be willing to watch our every step. We must be willing to pray to our merciful God that He blesses us with the memory of where our true joy is found: In honoring Him through seeking His will.

"Therefore, since we have a great High Priest Who has ascended into heaven, Jesus the Son of God, let us hold firmly to the faith we profess. For we do not have a High Priest Who is unable to empathize with our weaknesses, but we have One Who has been tempted in every way, just as we are—yet He did not sin. Let us then approach God's throne of grace with confidence, so that we may receive mercy and find grace to help us in our time of need" (Hebrews 4:14-16 NIV). May God's mercy draw us to His Throne when we sin. May we see His blessed Light descending from afar. May we watch as His Mercy rests upon our hearts like a dove. It is not that we deserve anything, but it is a recognition that we have everything. Christ loves the lost, and that is why He went to the Cross.

God turning away from the cry of ""*Eli, Eli, lemasabachthani?*" (which means "My God, My God, why have You forsaken Me?")" (Matthew 27:46 NIV) should make us sit in meditation, filled with tears. How could God not free His Son from the Cross? How could God look at the wickedness and ungodliness of mankind spitting, mocking, torturing, and tormenting His Son, and not smite man right then and there? It is mercy, my friend. It is mercy for His very creation. He knew we did nothing to deserve Him. Yet, His mercy is what turned His back on His own Son! Not only this, but it was also the mercy of the Son Who chose to remain upon that Cross. He felt every blow and agonizing pain that had been done to Him on His way to the Cross. He went through the worst death for the worst sinners in hopes of bringing them to the best place with the Holy One. It is Christ alone Whose lovingkindness was revealed through His merciful walk to the Cross.

When we find ourselves falling short, let us run to the mercy of God that has saved us from the clutches of Satan. It is God Who loves us, despite our imperfections. Christ knows our weaknesses. He knows we are fallible, finite beings of sinful inclinations. Nevertheless, He chooses to help us through this life as we progress down the road of righteousness through sanctification. "Who is a God like You, Who pardons sin and forgives the transgression of the remnant of His inheritance? You do not stay angry forever but delight to show mercy. You will again have compassion on us; You will tread our sins underfoot and hurl all our iniquities into the depths of the sea" (Micah 7:18-19 NIV).

May God's mercy be imprinted upon our minds. May this unfathomable truth motivate us to rest in the bosom of our Lord Jesus Christ. May we flee from sexual immorality and Satan's temptations. May we cling to the One Who loved us before we were given an earthly name. It is only by the merciful atoning sacrifice of Christ that we can know the Father. It is only through the Holy Spirit that this magnificent story's impact can be both multiplied and remembered through its simplicity and its complexity. It is only the Holy Spirit Who can reveal to us deeper revelations of what Christ truly did upon that Cross.

May the God of mercy sit upon the throne of our heart. May His mercy flow through us and touch those around us. Great is the God of mercy. He is worthy of praise.

* * *

HEAVENLY FATHER, we are sinners saved only by Your grace and mercy. We are not good in ourselves. We have done nothing to earn our salvation. Your mercy, O God, is beyond comprehension. Why You would choose to let Your

Son die for us wretched sinners is a truth that will be pondered throughout all eternity. Nevertheless, we accept Your mercy with all humility. Keep us on the right path, O God. Give us the strength to not sin against You. May Your mercy both motivate us to do what is right and to extend mercy to others. May the Holy Spirit's presence control our thoughts, words, motives, and actions to do that which is found right in Your sight. May Christ's Blood wash us clean. By Your mercy may the remembrance of our sins be erased. When we are tempted, may the feeling of how we felt after sinning the last time drive us to not do the very thing we are tempted of doing. May guilt and shame flee at the Cross, for You are the Lord Who saves the lost. May all come to know You, Father. We thank You for Your mercy. In Jesus' name, Amen.

QUOTES FOR MEDITATION

1. "Trust the past to the mercy of God, the present to His love, and the future to His providence." **Saint Augustine**
2. "No one is strong in his own strength, but he is safe by the grace and mercy of God." **Cyprian**
3. "We implore the mercy of God, not that He may leave us at peace in our vices, but that He may deliver us from them." **Blaise Pascal**
4. "There is more mercy in Christ than sin in us." **Richard Sibbes**
5. "God's mercy is so great that you may sooner drain the sea of its water, or deprive the sun of its light, or make space too narrow, than diminish the great mercy of God." **Charles Spurgeon**

JUSTICE

⁂

TO MAKE RIGHT

"*or we know Him Who said, "Vengeance is mine; I will repay." And again, "The Lord will judge His people."*"
— *Hebrews 10:30 ESV*

GOD'S JUSTICE reveals His faithfulness. He is not a God Who can lie, and He is the Protector of His children. He does not seek to make to destroy. He longs for everything in which He created to be perfect and pure. Though many may come to hear the Gospel, many will reject Its Truth. It grieves the heart of God when men choose to flee from the blessed gift of salvation. It saddens God when men choose their ways over Him. However, in His sadness there is anger and wrath. "For the LORD, Whose name is Jealous, is a jealous God" (Exodus 34:14 ESV). Those who choose to despise the gift of Jesus Christ that is given so graciously and freely, will receive the punishment of damnation for all eternity.

Multitudes today may believe that God cannot be a God of wrath, but it is in His justice that His wrath is made known. If God did not have boiling anger and wrath towards those who despise Him, reject Him, and bring harm to His children, then He would not be a God of love. For true love is found in justice. You cannot have justice without love. Likewise, you cannot have love without justice. As love calls all and seeks to harm none, justice brings forth appropriate punishment for what is wrongly done. "He judges the world with righteousness; He judges the peoples with uprightness" (Psalm 9:8 ESV). God judges in righteousness because He is Holy. Anything that contradicts the nature of holiness must be rightfully judged. If that which was done contradicts His holiness and it is not covered by the Blood of Christ, then it is to be judged in full. There is no mercy for those who reject the longsuffering and patient God. God must bring forth justice to "vindicate His people and have compassion on His servants." God does this when "He sees that their power is gone and there is none remaining, bond or free" (Deuteronomy 32:36 ESV).

All the murders, adulterers, fornicators, swindlers, idolaters, and wicked transgressors of every age will have justice brought to them by Almighty God Himself. They will not be able to stand against His justice, for God's justice is pure, righteous, and holy. It is the foundation in which all that is wrong will not go unpunished or excused. To allow harm and wrong to happen without punishment is to fail to do what is necessary: tough love. For the believer, we are chastised, convicted, and disciplined when we do that which is wrong. For the unbeliever, they are left without remorse (unless they have not been given over to a reprobate mind and God is still calling them to Him). God does not seek to chastise the unbeliever when they have forsaken His calling time and time again. He will let them flounder and fall and go their own way in this life.

Those who choose to live in the lust and pride of life will have their full reward of indulgence in this life. It will not be until they stand before the Judgment Seat that they will regret ignoring every drawing from the Holy Spirit. They will stand in fear of the One Who is Omnipotent and Sovereign. As God is ready to unhinge His wrath upon them, they will have no one to blame but themselves. There will be no voice to stand against God's wrath. For it is only Christ Who speaks, advocates, and intercedes for those who are found in Him. All others are doomed to a hopeless, eternal drifting from God in the Lake of Fire.

""For behold, the LORD will come in fire, and His chariots like the whirlwind, to render His anger in fury, and His rebuke with flames of fire. For by fire will the LORD enter into judgment, and by His sword, with all flesh; and those slain by the LORD shall be many"" (Isaiah 66:15-16 ESV). Many will perish by God's hand. Those who mocked and scoffed at God and those who persecuted Christians without repenting will be tormented beyond understanding. God's justice is not a *torture*. Rather, it is a *torment*. The Lake of Fire will be torturous, yes; but God will not have them *tortured* based upon what we know "torture" to be from our human vocabulary. The *torment* comes from the reality that the conscience will never die once it is found in the Lake of Fire. That is what will be the *torment* throughout all eternity. It is the continual knowing and reflecting on all the times that God provided opportunities for the ungodly to turn from their ways that they rejected. In and out of past conscious experiences will be the continual cycle of seeing missed opportunities on earth and being brought back into Hell in the Lake of Fire.

This is important to understand, for it is "by the fear of the LORD one turns away from evil" (Proverbs 16:6 ESV). Understanding God's coming wrath should excite the believer, but also burden their heart for a lost world. Those who refuse to know God have no clue what is to come. It is important for us to not be happy about seeing others go astray. Even though in Heaven we will be glad to see God cast the ungodly into the Lake of Fire, it is in this life that we should partake with God's longsuffering patience. We must pray that all would come to know Him and we must strive to share the Gospel with them. To sit idly by and wish damnation on someone is far from God's heart.

We must remember that the appalling acts of wrong that were done to us will not go unpunished. "For My eyes are on all their ways. They are not hidden from Me, nor is their iniquity concealed from My eyes" (Jeremiah 16:17 ESV). Just as God has a record of all those written in the Book of Life (Malachi 3:16-18), so He remembers the iniquities of the ungodly. They will not escape the coming Judgment. Even the ungodly will not remember everything wrong that they did, but God has every sinful word, action, and motive remembered. His coming wrath will be upon those who lived their lives in sin. Though there are many *kind* unbelievers in this life, there is no one who is *good*. For every good deed that is done, there are one thousand sins. We must warn unbelievers of the justice that is to come if they do not repent and believe that Jesus Christ is Lord and Savior.

""As I looked, thrones were placed, and the Ancient of Days took His seat; His clothing was white as snow, and the hair of His head like pure wool; His throne was fiery flames; its wheels were burning fire. A stream of fire issued and came out from before Him; a thousand thousands served Him, and ten thousand times ten thousand stood before Him; the court sat in judgment, and the books were opened" (Daniel 7:9-10 ESV). Our minds must remember this day is coming. The power that will be seen and felt will have us prostrated. We will be both in awe and fear as believers. We will not know what to say or do, for the power that will surround us will overwhelm us.

What a day it will be to see the King of kings bring justice to every man and woman of every generation. As time will be no more in eternity, we will have nowhere else to go. We will have no schedule but to wait our turn to be called by the Omniscient God. It is "on that day when, according to my gospel, God judges the secrets of men by Christ Jesus" (Romans 2:16 ESV). May we find no one in our life on the side of God's soul damning words, ""Depart from Me, you cursed, into the eternal fire prepared for the devil and his angels'"" (Matthew 25:41 ESV). May we share the Gospel to all in hopes that all will flee from the wrath that is to come.

Though many would argue that God has no right to do such a thing to a person, it is important to have a proper understanding and context. God will not have those who never wanted to know Him in this life spend an eternity with Him in the afterlife. Those who did not want to worship the One, True, Living God in this life will not want to worship Him in the afterlife. There is no justice found in saving someone who wants nothing to do with God. If we were to forgive a homeless man who killed our child and invite him to live into our house; if he rejects such a gift time and time again in this life, then he will permanently remain in his decision in the afterlife. There would be no change of mind in the next life for the homeless man to come and live with us. Similarly, it is with those who deny God. We may find this unfair, but we must understand that "the Lord is our judge; the Lord is our Lawgiver; the Lord is our King" (Isaiah 33:22 ESV).

The Lord created and established the laws of all things in order that we may live by them. God's "pre-eternal justice" in this life has produced consequences for sin. He did this in hopes of revealing to man that sin is the way to death and that there is no merit or gain in the long run. If He Who is Pure and Holy designed the moral laws of that which is good and evil, then He most certainly did so in order to show us the way towards Truth and Life. God is just as gracious in His willingness to show us the path towards what is good, as He is in bringing consequences for sin. Both are a means of drawing us to Him and having a living relationship with Him.

"They will give account to Him Who is ready to judge the living and the dead" (1 Peter 4:5 ESV). God's patience is longsuffering, but His justice stands ready to judge at any time. He is the Omnipotent and Immanent God. ""No creature is hidden from His sight, but all are naked and exposed to the eyes of Him to Whom we must give account" (Hebrews 4:13 ESV). Justice is only perfectly done by a Perfect Being. God is Perfect. It is His infinitude that transcends Him beyond all things to see all things. In seeing all things, God can judge all things. Justice in all realms of life is perfectly orchestrated by the brush of His omnipotent hand and omniscient mind. As God remembers all and can see all, He is able to judge all. For God alone is Justice Himself.

Let us go to Him Who stands between the gap of salvation and sin; Heaven and Hell; life and damnation. Let us find Christ while He may be found in this life. Let our cry in this life be "Oh, let the evil of the wicked come to an end, and may You establish the righteous— You Who test the minds and hearts, O righteous God" (Psalm 7:9 ESV), for in Heaven our cry will be "O Lord of hosts, Who judges righteously, Who tests the heart and the mind, let me see Your vengeance upon them, for to You have I committed my cause" (Jeremiah 11:20 ESV). We must commit to God's love now, in order that we may flee from His wrath to come.

God's perfect will is for all to know Him. However, He must bring vengeance to all sin and evil that is not forgiven through the Blood of Christ. May we give praise forever to Him Who, through love, brings justice. May we worship Him Who established the laws of life that we move and live by. May we thank Him for His willingness to show us the way to Everlasting Life.

It is by God's justice that mankind, Satan, and demons will be judged. Our Father in Heaven cannot be conquered. No mouth will change His mind. No act will dismantle Him. God stands in complete authority. Those who argue against His justice rob Him of His holiness. Let us therefore live our lives in the love of God as we remember that He is Just and will do that which must be done to remain faithful.

* * *

LORD JESUS, we thank You that You are the One and Only Judge Who is Pure and Perfect. Vengeance is Yours, O God. No man can stand against what You have already commanded. No demon can destroy what You will do. Lord, may all come to know You, in order that they may flee from Your coming wrath. If You are willing to save us, O Lord, then You are certainly willing to save those apart from You. For none of us are righteous, Father. Only You are Perfect and Pure and Holy. As we walk through this life, give us the grace to endure persecution. May we live a Christ-like life in this life, in order that all may come to know You. God, when we are brought into the afterlife, we will be confident that our salvation is in You and You alone. You are Just and we know we are Your children, through the Blood of Christ

Jesus. In the afterlife, we will give You praise as You cast Satan, demons, and all the unrepentant transgressors of all the ages into the Lake of Fire. Our hearts long for none to go there, but when the time comes, Father, we will be grateful. We will give You praise that Your perfect justice will be done. Mighty are You, O God of Justice. In Jesus' name, Amen.

QUOTES FOR MEDITATION

1. "There is justice in Hell, but sin is the most unjust thing. It would rob God of His glory, Christ of His purchase, the soul of its happiness." **Thomas Watson**
2. "The magnitude of the punishment matches the magnitude of the sin. Now a sin that is against God is infinite; the higher the person against whom it is committed, the graver the sin - it is more criminal to strike a head of state than a private citizen - and God is of infinite greatness. Therefore an infinite punishment is deserved for a sin committed against Him." **Thomas Aquinas**
3. "God's justice stands forever against the sinner in utter severity. The vague and tenuous hope that God is 'too kind' to punish the ungodly has become a deadly opiate for the consciences of millions. It hushes their fears and allows them to practice all pleasant forms of iniquity while death draws everyday nearer and the command to repent goes unregarded. As responsible moral beings, we dare not so trifle with our eternal future." **A.W. Tozer**
4. "Almost every natural man that hears of Hell, flatters himself that he shall escape it." **Jonathan Edwards**

5. "The wicked will gnaw their tongues for anguish and pain; they will curse God and look upwards. There the dogs of Hell, pride, malice, revenge, rage, horror, despair, continually devour them." **John Wesley**

WISDOM

QUALITY OF HAVING
EXPERIENCE & KNOWLEDGE;
APPLICATION OF KNOWLEDGE

"*It is He Who made the earth by His power, Who established the world by His wisdom, and by His understanding stretched out the heavens.*"
— *Jeremiah 10:12 ESV*

GOD IS the nucleus behind all wisdom. Wisdom resides within Him, and there is no wisdom that can be obtained outside of Him. He perceives and discerns perfectly, for He is the Untaught Person Who possesses that which is to be learned by all other beings. As wisdom is the application of knowledge, knowledge is knowing that which is. Wisdom, therefore, is knowing how to apply what is known, perfectly. Wisdom is following through and acting upon that which is known. Wisdom is intertwined with God's Word, for true wisdom comes from the Scriptures. It is wisdom that is planted within us by the Holy Spirit when we take the time to read His Holy Word and seek God's face. Wisdom is given graciously by God Himself to all who seek it. "If any of you lacks wisdom, let him ask God, Who gives generously to all without reproach, and it will be given him" (James 1:5 ESV).

God's wisdom is directly associated with omniscience. As knowledge is knowing what is, omniscience is knowing all that was, is, and shall be. God's wisdom is perfect because He is the only One Who knows all things. God Himself has already seen the future, for the future resides in Him. Therefore, God's wisdom operates based upon His omniscience. To know all things and what is to come gives God the ability to know what must be done perfectly to progress His plan and move His Kingdom forward.

The Lord does not need any of us, but He chooses to share with us His wisdom. "For the LORD gives wisdom; from His mouth come knowledge and understanding" (Proverbs 2:6 ESV). This wisdom knows the right words to say at any given time. It knows when a routine must be disrupted to help someone in need. It knows when to encourage and lift others up. It knows when to be kind and gentle, and when to be bold and courageous. God's wisdom resides within us when we have the Holy Spirit. By continually asking God to share His wisdom with us, we can grow in the knowledge of Him and productivity for Him.

""With God are wisdom and might; He has counsel and understanding"" (Job 12:13 ESV). God's wisdom channels through His omnipotence. It gives Him ultimate authority to do as needed. For that which needs to be done, will always be done by the Lord. Though we are finite beings, and many times miss God's voice and wisdom, God has the wisdom to bring forth additional opportunities and work through us in different ways. He is not a God Who is caught off guard when we make mistakes. He is the Divine One that knows exactly what to always do.

He arranges second chances and other opportunities of growth. His wisdom brings forth His might. His might is seen through His wisdom. He implants innovation, ideas, thoughts, and actions within the soul of a genuine convert. He can speak at any time, and He has full authority to speak in a variety of ways. To us who are born-again, we know that God's voice is not audible. It is not like talking to a person (though it can be at certain times). Instead, God's voice is an inner voice. His voice is the voice of the Holy Ghost within Who is always speaking to us.

It is a miraculous wonder that God is willing to share Himself with us. The Holy God is willing to speak to us and work through us. The celebrities of our day are too "intelligent" or "too busy" to deal with the average person. However, it is those who are marginalized by the world that God loves to work through the most. God will always humble the proud by raising up someone who is weak in their own strength (1 Corinthians 1:27). For God's wisdom sees each person as made in His image. God knows that those who are the weakest tend to be the humblest when it comes to knowing Christ. Those who have little and see themselves as wretched sinners in need of a Savior will usually submit their all to God. There will be no underlying, hidden self within. There will just be a heart that longs for Heaven and longs for God's will to be done. For God's wisdom is shared even to the weakest of the weak. He takes great joy in sharing His wisdom with those who are lowly in spirit and of a contrite heart.

"No wisdom, no understanding, no counsel can avail against the LORD" (Proverbs 21:30 ESV). There is no competition when a being created is compared to Thee Creator of all. As God created man through His wisdom and omniparience, He knew everything that was going to happen. God in His wisdom knew that man would turn against Him. God knew that some would try to fight Him and excuse Him from their minds. Those who would dare try to outsmart God are some of the highest ranked fools of our day. How can one outsmart his Creator? How can one plan to defeat God's purpose and plan? This type of thinking is like a bloody fish trying to cross a pool infested with sharks. To attempt to move along and excel beyond God's wisdom is to deny reason and fall prey to foolish pride and self-deception.

O the beauty found in Job 28:12-28 (ESV), as the foundations of wisdom and understanding are brought into light:

""But where shall wisdom be found? And where is the place of understanding? Man does not know its worth, and it is not found in the land of the living. The deep says, 'It is not in me,' and the sea says, 'It is not with me.' It cannot be bought for gold, and silver cannot be weighed as its price. It cannot be valued in the gold of Ophir, in precious onyx or sapphire. Gold and glass cannot equal it, nor can it be exchanged for jewels of fine gold. No mention shall be made of coral or of crystal; the price of wisdom is above pearls. The topaz of Ethiopia cannot equal it, nor can it be valued in pure gold. "From where, then, does wisdom come? And where is the place of understanding? It is hidden from the eyes of all living and concealed from the birds of the air. Abaddon and Death say, 'We have heard a rumor of it with our ears.' "God understands the way to it, and He knows its place. For He looks to the ends of the earth and sees everything under the heavens. When He gave to the wind its weight and apportioned the waters by measure, when He made a decree for the rain and a way for the lightning of the thunder, then He saw it and declared it; He established it, and searched it out. And He said to man, 'Behold, the fear of the Lord, that is wisdom, and to turn away from evil is understanding.""

God's wisdom brought forth life! God's wisdom developed the pathways and operations behind every living thing. God channeled His wisdom through His creation. Look around and see the miraculous wonder of how everything works! See creation move on this earth. See the seas roar and lightning fall from the sky! Everything is operated by God in perfect harmony.

Nature is the beauty of God's wisdom that is visible, whereas we are beings who can make God's wisdom applicable. As God created us, He made us in hopes that we would seek after Him and His wisdom. "The fear of the LORD is the beginning of wisdom, and the knowledge of the Holy One is insight" (Proverbs 9:10 ESV). The fear of God is to possess a holy hatred for sin. When we no longer seek our sin over God, that is when the barriers of a hardened heart crumble. It is by fearing God that He touches us with wisdom that transcends human understanding.

To fear the Lord also means to not live in a state of perpetual questioning. "Then Job answered and said: "Truly I know that it is so: But how can a man be in the right before God? If one wished to contend with Him, one could not answer Him once in a thousand times. He is wise in heart and mighty in strength —who has hardened himself against Him, and succeeded?" (Job 9:1-4 ESV). Why must we question and demand answers from Him Who holds wisdom? If God has allowed something, does He not know the appropriate time to act? Will He not show us what must be done at the right time?

O how great is the ultimate wisdom found in simple rest. Waiting upon God is wisdom. For it does not look within oneself. Rather, it seeks the perfect wisdom that rests in the heavenly realm. As the soul rests, the Holy Spirit abides and rises within. He is the One Who reaches out to the Father and grasps wisdom (1 Corinthians 2:10-15). It is the Holy Spirit Who enlightens and brings forth supernatural peace, by bestowing within our heart quiet wisdom. This quiet wisdom is not seen in plain sight. Instead, it is hidden. As we move quietly throughout each day waiting upon the Lord, it is God Who has already given us the wisdom in advance. Through preparing the heart to seek the Lord, He gives us Divine wisdom. He gives us the wisdom of knowing how to act and be according to the Scriptures. It is then in Christ "in Whom are hidden all the treasures of wisdom and knowledge" (Colossians 2:3 ESV).

When we know what is requested and what must be done according to God's wisdom, our quiet wisdom becomes publicly known. This wisdom is different from the world's, for even "the foolishness of God is wiser than men, and the weakness of God is stronger than men" (1 Corinthians 1:25 NKJV). This wisdom is selfless and comes from a softened heart. Once sensitivity to the Spirit's voice has been met, one is able to not only hear but enact upon God's instruction. It is James 3:13-18 (NKJV) that reveals what wisdom from the world looks like, and what wisdom from God looks like:

"Who *is* wise and understanding among you? Let him show by good conduct *that* his works *are done* in the meekness of wisdom. But if you have bitter envy and self-seeking in your hearts, do not boast and lie against the truth. This wisdom does not descend from above, but *is* earthly, sensual, demonic. For where envy and self-seeking *exist,* confusion and every evil thing *are* there. But the wisdom that is from above is first pure, then peaceable, gentle, willing to yield, full of mercy and good fruits, without partiality and without hypocrisy. Now the fruit of righteousness is sown in peace by those who make peace."

O how perfect and pure is the wisdom that comes from the Holy One! How we should despise the worldly wisdom that would dare try to infiltrate our minds. We must not allow such carnality to touch our soul. It is God Who is wisdom, and it is us who must seek Him. We must despise worldly wisdom at all costs. We must ascend our soul to the realm where no physical being may go. Although Heaven will never be seen in this life, thanks be to God that Heaven is able to come to us. As the Holy Spirit comes, He brings forth grace, gentleness, mercy, good fruits, humility, and love. We must allow our faith to "not rest in the wisdom of men but in the power of God" (1 Corinthians 2:5 ESV). For "His Divine power has granted to us all things that pertain to life and godliness, through the knowledge of Him Who called us to His own glory and excellence" (2 Peter 1:3 ESV).

What a tragedy it is to be enthralled and infatuated with the world. How infinite our God is! How willing He is to give, yet we choose to neglect His wisdom! "Woe to those who go down to Egypt for help and rely on horses, who trust in chariots because they are many and in horsemen because they are very strong, but do not look to the Holy One of Israel or consult the LORD! And yet He is wise and brings disaster; He does not call back His words, but will arise against the house of the evildoers and against the helpers of those who work iniquity" (Isaiah 31:1-2 ESV). How mighty is God! How great is His wisdom to know when justice must be done.

God will not sit by and watch His people be mocked and persecuted for long. Though it may seem long to us, there is a day of retribution that is sure to come. God's wisdom knew that such a place as Hell and the Lake of Fire needed to be created. In His wisdom, He created such places for Satan and his demons (Matthew 25:41). Those who go in the way of demons will be numbered amongst all the ungodly and wicked transgressors of all the ages.

Since God possesses all wisdom, He therefore cannot learn anything new. "Whom did He consult, and who made Him understand? Who taught Him the path of justice, and taught Him knowledge, and showed Him the way of understanding? Behold, the nations are like a drop from a bucket, and are accounted as the dust on the scales; behold, He takes up the coastlands like fine dust" (Isaiah 40:14-15 ESV). All the world's wisdom does not compare to one dose of holy wisdom from On High. Thoughts, plans, and strategies are nothing compared to Him Who possesses all, works through all, and knows all. It is to our benefit to know these truths. Greater still is our willingness to stop relying on our wisdom. "The horse is made ready for the day of battle, but the victory belongs to the Lord" (Proverbs 21:31 ESV).

We can only think of so many ideas. We can only create so many opportunities. It is God's sovereignty that has the final say on whether something should be allowed. Why should we try to create and do that which is contrary to Him? He is Thee All-Wise God (Romans 16:27)! It is to our benefit to lay down our own resources and selfishness and seek the face of God. It is fulfilling to stop asking the world and others their thoughts and opinions, and to begin to seek God's counsel first. Once we have received a Word from God and gone to Him first, then we are able to act appropriately and ask others for their insight.

We must not depend upon man, but upon God solely for deliverance, guidance, wisdom, and strength! "Now to Him Who is able to strengthen you according to my gospel and the preaching of Jesus Christ, according to the revelation of the mystery that was kept secret for long ages but has now been disclosed and through the prophetic writings has been made known to all nations, according to the command of the eternal God, to bring about the obedience of faith—to the only wise God be glory forevermore through Jesus Christ! Amen" (Romans 16:25-27 ESV).

* * *

LORD JESUS, we thank You for Your wisdom that is readily accessible at any point in time. Lord, we thank You that You are gracious enough to share wisdom from On High to those who are found in You. We thank You that Your wisdom has brought us salvation through Christ and justice for the wicked who do not turn from their ways. Your wisdom, O Lord, can deliver us from any sin, circumstance, or confusion. Lord, may our souls be still and know that You are God. May we receive Your wisdom and apply it within our lives. Thank You, Lord, for Your Holy Spirit. May He continue to show us, guide us, and mold us into warriors for Christ. It is to our benefit that we seek You in all things. For You alone, O God, know all things. May we not become lazy, stagnant, or seek counsel from that which is outside of You. Rather, may we become creatures of habit. May we choose to go to You the moment we are distressed, worried, and unsure. You, O Lord, are worthy of praise. Great are You to share wisdom to those Who ask. We bless You, Father. In Jesus' name, Amen.

QUOTES FOR MEDITATION

1. "But if you search further, you find in yourself nothing similar to God, but rather you affirm that God stands above all this as Cause, Origin, and the Light of life of your intellective soul." **Nicholas of Cusa**
2. "May the strength of God pilot us, may the wisdom of God instruct us, may the hand of God protect us, may the Word of God direct us. Be always ours this day and for evermore." **Saint Patrick**
3. "But the Wisdom of God, which is His only-begotten Son, being in all respects incapable of change or alteration, and every good quality in Him being essential, and such as cannot be changed and converted, His glory is therefore declared to be pure and sincere." **Origen**
4. "If Christ is the wisdom of God and the power of God in the experience of those who trust and love Him, there needs no further argument of His Divinity." **Henry Ward Beecher**
5. "God doth not govern the world only by His will as an absolute monarch, but by His wisdom and goodness as a tender father. It is not His greatest pleasure to show His

sovereign power, or His inconceivable wisdom, but His immense goodness, to which He makes the other attributes subservient." **Stephen Charnock**

PERFECTION

$$\mathcal{S}$$

PURE; FAULTLESS; FLAWLESS

""*The Rock, His work is perfect, for all His ways are justice. A God of faithfulness and without iniquity, just and upright is He.""*
— *Deuteronomy 32:4 ESV*

GOD OPERATES PERFECTLY because He Himself is perfect. There is nothing higher than the blessed perfection of the Lord Jesus Christ. Within Him all virtues flow. There is no being more perfect than God Himself. He is perfect in Who He is and in what He does. There is no person greater than God in Heaven. He is perfect in all His ways. His unwavering Person keeps Him as He is, so long as He is. There is no evil that comes from His Being. There are no mistakes that are made when He moves. In God alone does all perfection flow. Only in Him can the beauty of life be found and obtained.

"This God—His way is perfect; the word of the Lord proves true; He is a shield for all those who take refuge in Him" (2 Samuel 22:31 ESV). When God's perfection falls upon His children, He becomes their Protector and Shield from the enemy. If we slip and fall, God does not cast us aside. Rather, His perfect counsel directs us back to

Him in repentance. By His perfect discipline our hearts are changed to seek after perfection and holiness once again; even if it cannot be fully attained until we are in Heaven.

God perfectly disciplines His children in love and gentleness. Though this gentleness may be felt with deep conviction, it nonetheless is done with a gentle Spirit. For it is the Holy Spirit that speaks to us and gives us the understanding of Who our Perfect Father is. He is the One Who sent His Perfect Spirit to live inside these imperfect vessels. God's willingness to place His perfection into someone who contradicts His perfection reveals to mankind that He is a God of perfect love. He is willing to come down to our level, to help us come up to His. Though His perfection be in a dimension of its own, perfection as we understand it can be obtained through the Holy Spirit's working in us. For as we see that we are undeserving of such a powerful, gentle Spirit within us, so we should naturally press into the perfect love of God and seek His perfect will.

To know God's perfect will, we must know His perfect Word. "The words of the Lord are pure words, like silver refined in a furnace on the ground, purified seven times" (Psalm 12:6 ESV). Though God speaks to us in many ways, He Himself has left us His perfect Word through the Scriptures. It is in His written Word that we find His perfection. We see His dealings with the ungodly, as well as those who are lowly. We see how Perfection Himself was crucified. We see how Christ had to bear the weight of all sin and wickedness upon that Cross.

It is to no surprise that our Perfect God can be seen through His Word. For He is the Perfect Author Who blessed the minds of men to write that which He knew would be established and passed down from generation to generation. Without God's Word today, we would have trouble understanding Who He is and what His perfect will is. Though we have the Spirit, it is essential to have both the Holy Spirit and The Holy Bible. For both give guidance and clarity. Without the Holy Spirit, the Bible would be just another book. Likewise, without the Holy Bible we would not be able to understand exactly Who the Holy Spirit is. It takes One to know the Other. Many lifetimes could be spent attempting to understand them both without fully coming to understand them. The Holy Bible will forever speak to us and bring forth revelations. Likewise, the Holy Spirit will forever be the Mystery that shall never be *fully* comprehended, even though His gentle voice be heard within our inner being.

"You therefore must be perfect, as your Heavenly Father is perfect" (Matthew 5:48 ESV). We must seek after perfection. As we stand before our Perfect Father on that Final Day, we ourselves will be found perfect alone by the Blood of the Lord Jesus Christ. Though we ourselves are not perfect and never will be in our own strength, it is the Perfect Son Who implants His Cross upon our chest and says, "Father, this one is found in Me." It is in the willingness of a Perfect Savior to die for an imperfect people that perfect love, grace, and mercy is seen. To take an unholy person out of an unholy world and give them the Holy Spirit is one of the most beautiful displays of God's perfection.

It is the Holy Spirit Who sanctifies us along the path of holiness. Though the word "Holy" solely belongs to God, it is the striving after holiness that transforms us and prepares us to be in His presence. As *holiness* is perfect purity, *perfection* is the nature and persona of that which is acceptable and appropriate in all given circumstances. It is the Holy Spirit that leads us down the path of holiness. It is the Blood of Christ that makes us perfect. Both are undeserved, but we accept Both with all humility. For without Each of Them, we would not be that which God longs for us to be.

God's perfection lives within and comes to fruition at various points within our walk. The times in which we may be temporarily perfect is mostly found in prayer. "Do not be conformed to this world, but be transformed by the renewal of your mind, that by testing you may discern what is the will of God, what is good and acceptable and perfect" (Romans 12:2 ESV). Prayer is the most powerful form of perfection that we will obtain in this life. It is prayer that calls upon the Perfect One. It is prayer that renews our mind and reveals to us what is of God and what is not of God. When prayer is directed by the Holy Spirit and aided by the Scriptures, we become free from distraction. We can pray perfectly and know the heart of God when we have nothing but that which is led by God Himself. It takes God to pray to God, and this is where a dose of perfection can be found.

As we submit ourselves to the Perfect Holy Spirit, we partake in the perfect transmission of prayers to our Perfect Heavenly Father. We are a continued, progressing vessel in this life. However, it is the Perfect One Who makes us perfect during very brief moments throughout this life. This perfection is just a dose of the jubilation and goodness that is to come. We are only given subtle hints of the Heavenly realm when we walk and keep in step with the Spirit. O how it is a blessed gift to be continually transformed into holy citizens for God in this life, until we reach pure perfection in the afterlife!

By continually focusing on God's perfection, we are motivated and compelled to be like Him. "Since we have these promises, beloved, let us cleanse ourselves from every defilement of body and spirit, bringing holiness to completion in the fear of God" (2 Corinthians 7:1 ESV). As we focus on God's perfection, we naturally possess a mindset that longs after perfection, holiness, and righteousness. Focusing on Who God is and who we are not allows us to possess a holy fear of God. When we stand in reverence at His power, His glory, and His perfection, we are brought to a place that seeks nothing else but to glorify Him Who has given us all things. He is a God that gives good and perfect gifts at perfect times. If He did not do so in His perfect timing, then we would fall prey to becoming prideful or distancing ourselves from God. We would begin to rely on ourselves, rather than on Thee Perfect One. For our Heavenly Father is the God of perfect gifts and perfect timing, but His perfection is not limited there. It is in God's Law that His perfection is also seen.

"The law of the Lord is perfect, reviving the soul; the testimony of the Lord is sure, making wise the simple; the precepts of the Lord are right, rejoicing the heart; the commandment of the Lord is pure, enlightening the eyes; the fear of the Lord is clean, enduring forever; the rules of the Lord are true, and righteous altogether. More to be desired are they than gold, even much fine gold; sweeter also than honey and drippings of the honeycomb. Moreover, by them is your servant warned; in keeping them there is great reward" (Psalm 19:7-11 ESV). God is the only Being Who knows the difference between good and evil and remains unimpacted by its knowledge. He is the only One that has not fallen away from Good, for He is Good and Perfect. It is the knowledge and power of the Perfect One that has ordained and declared what is good and what is evil. For it is His Perfect Mind that knows what is perfect.

As God knows what is perfect because He Himself is Perfect, He knows what contradicts His nature. God knows what is unacceptable and is not of His Nature. As God knows, so He declares. In His written Word can be found what is good and perfect, and what is sinful and evil. There is no guessing or wondering of what perfection looks like. For perfection is simply God. He alone has been, is, and forever will remain Perfect.

God's perfection is also in His knowledge of knowing us. "O Lord, You have searched me and known me! You know when I sit down and when I rise up; You discern my thoughts from afar. You search out my path and my lying down and are acquainted with all my ways. Even before a word is on my tongue, behold, O Lord, You know it alto-gether. You hem me in, behind and before, and lay Your hand upon me. Such knowledge is too wonderful for me; it is high; I cannot attain it" (Psalm 139:1-6 ESV). God's knowledge is too high for us to obtain simply because we ourselves were created from that hidden knowledge. Since God made us according to His will, and since we know that His will is perfect, we can be sure that we were created without mistake. God purposely created us with purposeful intent. Since God does not redo, but always does, He Himself is perfect in how He creates.

God's perfection does not stop at creating, however. As God creates perfectly, He Himself knows perfectly. God knows both where we go and when we go. God knows what we say, before it is said. God knows our thoughts before we think them. God knows everything before it happens. Since God's foreknowledge is found within His omniscience, God is perfectly aware of knowing all things. Since God is omnipresent and forever everywhere, He perfectly sees all things.

There is not a being that can compete with God's perfect knowledge. There is nothing that can escape His perfect presence. God is always perfectly everywhere. It is in His Being that all things reside. With such power attached to His Holiness, Love, and Justice, He is perfect in whatever He does.

How magnificent it is to know that God not only created us perfectly in His image, He also created all else perfectly. As we see people pass by, God chose to place those people within the same generation as us. As we see animals and sea creatures move across the land and sea, God perfectly placed those animals within their given environment. Everything that is seen by the human eye was made from God's omniscient mind. God perfectly arranged for us to live in the time we are in, in order that we may come to know Him. God does not plant someone in the wrong time where we would be less likely to know Him. God sovereignly gives all people He creates in His image the best possible time of being born, with the best possible sources, within a particular environment to come to know Him throughout their journey of life.

God's perfection cannot be questioned, for there is no one who can transcend His infinitude or His omnibenevolence. It is in His transcendence that all His attributes descend. As He is the Highest, Unending Peak of all things, so His perfection rests within the Transcendent Realm that is unknown to all. We can trust that if God is for us and longs for all to come to Him (2 Peter 3:9, 1 Timothy 2:4), He will have placed people at the perfect time and place. He has done this that all might come to know Him Who is The Perfect One.

O how striking is the glorious truth that there is not one attribute of God that is imperfect! Every one of God's attributes make up God Himself, for He is the Attributes Themselves. He is not made up of that which makes Him up, directly. Rather, He gives meaning and reasoning to each attribute of His since they have always been with Him. God simply Is that which He Is, and in Him is all perfection. Therefore, we must never worry about God changing. For He will forever remain immutable!

As God is not able to change, He therefore will remain perfect in

Who He is. He is the Source of all Life, Knowledge, and Truth. It is our Lord Jesus Christ Who is "the Way, and the Truth, and the Life" (John 14:6 ESV). It is Christ Who is the Truth that provides the way that leads to Life. It is the distinct Persons of the Trinity that fulfill their economic roles of salvation, perfectly; while still remaining Unified and as One God. They are the Omnipotent Godhead; the Three in One. Within each Person of the Trinity, God's perfection is displayed. All Three have shown us the path of righteousness. All Three play an essential role in transforming us into perfect, holy saints of God.

Blessed be our Perfect God, Who does not change and does not waiver. Blessed be Him Who longs for us to become perfect, just as He is Perfect.

* * *

HEAVENLY FATHER, how Perfect and Holy You are. You are that which our hearts and souls strive for. We long to be perfect, just as You are Perfect. Lord, grow us in Your Perfection. Continue to sanctify us and distance us from that which is imperfect. Lord, may our soul and spirit be led by the Holy Spirit. May He show us the way and make it known to us. It is Your perfect will that we want to follow, Heavenly Father. It is Your perfect love that we want to press into and experience. It is Your perfect Law that we want to obey. It is Your perfect Son, Father, Whom we long to give eternal praise and worship. Blessed be You, O God, Who is perfect in every way. We rest in the knowledge of Your immutability. We allow the truth of Your omnibenevolence and perfection to take root within our hearts. You alone are our Perfect God. We praise You and lift Your Name High. In Jesus' name, Amen.

QUOTES FOR MEDITATION

1. "It is the perfection of God's works that they are all done with the greatest simplicity. He is the God of order and not of confusion. And therefore as they would understand the frame of the world must endeavor to reduce their knowledge to all possible simplicity, so must it be in seeking to understand these visions." **Isaac Newton**
2. "Christ is the most perfect image of God, into which we are so renewed as to bear the image of God, in knowledge, purity, righteousness, and true holiness." **John Calvin**
3. "We worship Unity in Trinity, and Trinity in Unity; neither confounding the Person nor dividing the Substance. There is One Person of the Father, Another of the Son, and Another of the Holy Ghost; but the Godhead of the Father, and of the Son, and of the Holy Ghost, is all One; the glory equal, the majesty co-eternal." **Tertullian**
4. "Moved by the perfection of His holy love, God in Christ substituted Himself for us sinners. That is the heart of the cross of Christ." **John Stott**
5. "When we become incorruptible and immortal, and attain to the blessed state of conformity with Christ, we will be

ever with the Lord (as Scripture says), gaining fulfillment in the purest contemplations of His visible theophany which will illuminate us with its most brilliant rays, just as it illuminated the Disciples at the time of the most Divine Transfiguration." **Gregory Palamas**

CONCLUSION

"We make assertions and denials of what is next to [the Divine Nature], but never of It, for It is both beyond every assertion, being the perfect and unique cause of all things, and, by virtue of Its preeminently simple and absolute nature, free of every limitation, beyond every limitation; it is also beyond every denial."
— ***Pope Dionysius***

God is the Inexhaustible Being Whose attributes are inapprehensible. He is the Master and Author of Life. He is the Orchestrator of unerring ways. He is the Transcendent Being of all Infallible Truth. He is the Immortal One Who will forever remain insurmountable. It is our God in Heaven Who eternally and infinitely transcends all. Though He remains Immutable, He remains Omnipotent, Omniscient, and Sovereign. Though He shares with us hidden secrets of His Nature, He Himself is beyond that which is shared. As we have gathered and observed each attribute of God, we must understand that complete and perfect justice of each attribute has not been done. Though it is concrete according to the Scriptures, it is not that which is complete in full understanding.

Though Scripture *describes* God, even His Word does not *fully* portray each attribute. For His Word was made for finite people. There are deeper truths to be learned in the afterlife. We must simply know that if each attribute were a grain of sand, we have simply picked up a grain from amidst a sandy beach. We know not its full understanding. For the Truthful knowledge of God that has been given through the Scriptures is not all there is; though, it is all Truth in this life. For even though the Holy Bible reveals God and His attributes, He remains *fully* unknown.

Looking at God's Word is like looking at a tunnel. We may see God's attributes as the overarching structure of the tunnel. However, we do not know its full extent or how far those attributes really go when viewing and understanding their meaning and application. It takes God to bring us Truth that is complete within our given realm. God cannot lie. Therefore, His Word cannot lie in what It teaches. God has chosen to bring Himself down to our understanding in hopes that we might pick up that grain of sand and know it as best as we can.

Once we ascend into Heaven, we will forever be complete in the Lord, but we will never *fully* know Him. This is the fascination and complexity of God that is so profound that we cannot begin to contemplate that which we do not know. For what we do not know is that which we cannot know to contemplate. One billion years in Heaven will have grown us infinitely wiser regarding Who God is. That place in which we come too, however, will be like knowing the number "2" in the entire, infinite numerical system. As we will be a million-fold wiser in our understanding of God a billion years in eternity, we ourselves right now cannot contemplate that which will be learned at that given point.

This is the mystery that keeps one engaged and excited with the glory and joy that is to come. For although being with our Lord Jesus Christ will be enough, the deepening of revelations of God Almighty Himself should also excite the soul. As we shall be at rest in Christ's presence once in Heaven, we will at the same time come to know God in greater understanding.

Let us thank the Lord for illuminating our soul with a touch from

Heaven. Let us give praise for the growth that has been derived from this reading. Though it is written by mere man, it nonetheless was a desire that was birthed to reveal just a dose of Who God is. The God which we now know will be the same God in eternity. However, this book will be but a sentence in the Bible of the knowledge that is to come. For it is God Who is The Unknown Known. It is the Father Who will forever remain Preeminent and Omnipotent. It is our Lord Jesus Christ Who will forever be the Immutable, Perfect Son of love, grace, mercy, faithfulness, and justice. It is the Holy Spirit Who will forever be the Mystery of mysteries. It is the Godhead that infinitely transcends finite comprehension. It is the Trinity that will forever remain inscrutable and incomprehensible! Great is the Trinity of Aseity! Mighty is our Incorporeal God! For it is God Who possesses and gives life to all things.

May we forever pursue the Ineffable God of *Ineffable Attributes*, until He calls us Home to reside with Him for all eternity. In the words of Gregory Palamas from *The Triads*, may our heart, mind, soul, and spirit forever seek "the very Kingdom of God, eternal and endless, the very light beyond intellection and unapproachable, the heavenly and infinite light, out of time and eternal, the light that makes immortality shine forth, the light which deifies those who contemplate it."

"To the only God, our Savior, through Jesus Christ our Lord, be glory, majesty, dominion, and authority, before all time and now and forever" (Jude 1:25 ESV). "To the King of the ages, immortal, invisible, the only God, be honor and glory forever and ever. Amen" (1 Timothy 1:17 ESV).

THANK YOU

I appreciate you taking the time to read through *Ineffable Attributes.* I hope it was beneficial to your growth in the Trinitarian God.

If this was a blessing, it would be greatly appreciated if you took a few minutes to write a review on Amazon.

An *honest* review can go a long way and can help make the book more visible to future audiences.

If you feel led to do so, I truly do thank you.

Judah Veritas

Author

LET'S CONNECT

If you would like to connect with Judah Veritas, you can find him on the following platforms:

For All Relevant Social Media, Linktree: https://linktr.ee/judahandjackieveritas

For Judah's Services: https://stan.store/ascendwithveritas

ABOUT JUDAH VERITAS

Judah Veritas came to a more profound knowledge of God when he realized it was only Jesus Christ Who could break the chains of sin that kept him bound.

He is passionate about diving deeper into the study of Who God is, His Attributes, His Nature, and His Being, and sharing the revelations he has received with all who have an ear to hear. His desire is for others to know God intimately. Not only as Father, Son, and Holy Spirit, but as Creator of the Universe.

His testimony is impactful, as it reveals God as the Deliverer. He was supernaturally set free from an addiction to pornography and masturbation at age 23, as a Non-Denominational Christian, and received the gift of tongues and discerning of spirits upon getting married.

Since the age of 25, Judah has consistently posted one video each day on YouTube containing apologetic, theological, or philosophical insight. He is an Entrepreneur, dedicated Author, husband to his wife, Jackie Veritas.

ALSO BY JUDAH VERITAS

Judah has multiple books in the works expected to launch this year and in the years ahead.

Ineffable Attributes is his first book. Others that are expected to come pertain to God (His Nature and Being), exposing false prophets and false gospels, the importance of the inner life as a Christian, the way of a true born-again believer, his personal testimony, and much more.

Some of the books that are to be released soon (or are already out) that were mentioned throughout *Ineffable Attributes* include:

- *The Forever Unknown*
- *The Unknown Known*
- *Unraveling Deception*

Be sure to stay in touch with his social for updates on upcoming books.

We hope **Ineffable Attributes** was an edifying read and was beneficial to your growth in the King of kings and Lord of lords.

God bless you, keep you, guide you, and continue to lead you in His Will, according to His Word.

www.ingramcontent.com/pod-product-compliance
Lightning Source LLC
Chambersburg PA
CBHW062045080426
42734CB00012B/2565